BROTHERS AND SISTERS

BROTHERS AND SISTERS

Discovering the Psychology of Companionship

Lara Newton

Spring Journal Books
New Orleans, Louisiana

Published by
Spring Journal, Inc.
627 Ursulines Street #7
New Orleans, Louisiana 70116
Tel.: (504) 524-5117
Website: www.springjournalandbooks.com

Cover design by
Northern Cartographic
4050 Williston Road
South Burlington, VT 05403

Cover art by
Jack Ruddy

Photograph on back cover by
Alexandra Sheremet

Printed in Canada
Text printed on acidfree paper

Library of Congress Cataloging-in-Publication Data Pending

For

my brother John
and my two children,
Jack and Madeleine,
who have all taught me about
companionship

Contents

Acknowledgments

Over the years, many clients, friends and near-strangers have graciously shared their brother-sister stories with me. Whether or not all the stories appear in the pages of this book, each has made a lasting impression on me and my work. I am humbled and grateful in the presence of such sharing.

All of the analysts with whom I shared my own life story have helped me transform my personal experience of the brother-sister relationship. First and foremost, Linda Leonard believed in me and in the value of my story at a crucial point in my young adulthood. Years later, she offered suggestions for this manuscript in its early stages, and she continues to encourage my creative life. I also owe a debt of gratitude to John Hill, Don Williams, and Jean Carlson.

I began writing on this topic in 1990. From those early days, I wish to thank Eugene Monick, Marilyn Matthews, and Mary Ann Mattoon, each of whom contributed in his or her own way to the development of my ideas.

My colleagues on the board of the Jung Institute of Colorado have been a long-standing support: Gary Toub, Jean Carlson, Glen Carlson, Annie Meyer, Bernice Hill, and Steve Witty. In fact, we provide such a firm and dependable container for each other's ideas and projects that the group hardly feels like a "board"—more like a family.

I wish to give special thanks to the members of the C. G. Jung Society of Colorado. They are a fine group of interested, intelligent individuals, and my first formal lecture on the brother-sister relationship was to that group.

What would life be without friends? My friend Debby Hiestand has encouraged and prodded me to keep writing, and all those pep talks over breakfast have been more help than she can imagine. Another friend, Minnie Baldwin, not only encouraged me, but revealed a hidden talent. She is an editor of extraordinary skill, and has been so generous with her time that I will truly never be able to repay her.

I am very grateful to Spring Journal Books and Nancy Cater, who is insightful, supportive, and easy to communicate with. I know how lucky I am to have met her.

Finally, my husband Steve is such a life-line for me that I could never say enough about how important he has been in the writing of this book. He is genuinely interested in my ideas, loves to listen and talk to me when I am working through a thorny or complicated concept, and can sense when I need solitude instead of talk. His faith in my work has never wavered.

L.N.

Foreword

When Lara Newton first told me of her plan to write a book on "Brothers and Sisters," I was delighted. How strange, I thought, that so little has been written on this topic when so many women and men come into therapy to deal with the rage and the tears, with the longings and the frustrations, as well as with the joys and the inspiration related to their siblings. Even those who have no siblings often long to have brothers and sisters and many turn to imagination for that special form of companionship. Whether or not we have outer siblings, sisters and brothers are frequent figures in our dreams and inner lives. And, archetypal motifs of the brother-sister relationship abound in films, literature, opera, art, myths and fairytales emphasizing the universality of this unique form of relationship throughout the history, religions, and various cultures of our human world.

How important, then, that Lara Newton has taken up this challenge. She shares with us her reflections on some of her own dreams and experiences with her personal brother, the struggles of her clients and other men and women, and in particular the ways in which fairy tales illumine various aspects of the psychology of siblings. Through her insightful analyses of fairy tales, her therapeutic knowledge as a Jungian Analyst, and her clear and lively writing style, Lara helps us understand both the creative and destructive tensions inherent in the sister-brother relationship. She takes us deep into this area of the psyche by elucidating crucial issues such as psychological incest, enchantment, abandonment, abuse, redemption, and reconciliation. She points the way to inner and outer transformation in her analysis of the developmental stages of bonding, wounding, and healing between bothers and sisters.

For more than thirty years, I have continued to enjoy and learn from the gift of the creative growth of sisterhood with Lara. I particularly appreciate her notion of the transformational "questing spirit" required by both sisters and brothers for their outer and inner growth. I also appreciate Lara's emphasis on the work of healing and redemption in the brother-sister relationship as an archetypal model for healthy life with each other in the world.

Linda Schierse Leonard, Ph.D.
2006

INTRODUCTION

A Sister's Story

The relationship I had with my brother as a child was more significant to me than any other relationship. My mother tells a story of bringing me home from the hospital as a newborn. My brother, then two years old, ran to the car, and my mother thought he was running to her. But he ran right past her open arms to the little baby next to her. From that day on, we were a team. "One lies and the other swears to it!" our mother would say, sometimes frustrated at our fierce loyalty to each other.

As I went through childhood, my brother was the person to whom I turned with my questions, fears, and hopes, and he turned to me as well. As children we stumbled or frolicked through the questions together. We created fantasies, never holding each other back or concerning ourselves with the usefulness or truthfulness of those fantasies. I don't suppose I ever expected him to have the knowledge or the absolute authority of my parents; we were only two years apart. But I did expect him to understand me better than the adult world could, and he did.

The first dream I recall vividly was when I was five, a fairytale-type dream in which my brother and I were companions in a mysterious adventure. Later, in my twenties, a week before I met my first Jungian analyst, I had another dream in which my brother and I were again companions, this time struggling against a dark and evil opponent. By this time, my brother and I led quite separate lives in the outer world—our paths had not been the same—but, as the dream indicated, in my inner world he continued to be by my side.

Throughout my life, profound dreams in which my brother is a major character have pointed the way toward transformational experiences which brought me to a new way of seeing and understanding myself and the world around me. As a young woman, before ever beginning analysis, I knew intuitively that this relationship and these dreams had a special significance for me. Now, as an older woman and a trained Jungian analyst, I have come to recognize the powerful psychological energy to which "brother" has connected me during my life.

Fairy tales, novels, poetry, famous brother-sister pairs, as well as clients who have come to me with their own brother-sister stories— all these, also, have contributed to my expanding awareness of the brother-sister relationship that dwells in the human heart and calls us to a new level of psychological development. Each time I have spoken on this topic, I have been struck by the strong responses I receive. Women and men alike begin to share their brother-sister stories and to open up an aspect of their lives that had been waiting to be heard. They respond with enthusiasm when I say that the relationship needs to be examined in its own right.

I sense that there is a world of brothers and sisters out there just waiting to be "understood" as such in addition to being understood as sons, daughters, husbands, wives, fathers, and mothers. Some may never have had a sibling, but they have experienced the brother-sister dynamic in their lives in other forms, such as a close relationship with a friend of the opposite sex, a fantasy relationship with a brother or sister, or perhaps through these figures appearing in their dream lives. These people are experiencing the living presence of the brother-sister pair as a psychological reality in the objective world. It is a universal and powerful experience. It is also an experience that is vitally important in our world today. Communication across the gender line is problematic at best, and if we expand the psychological meaning of "masculine" and "feminine," as Jung did, to encompass the two complementary modes of expression—doing and being, going forth and putting down roots—we can see how very necessary it is for us to communicate. Brother and sister provide us with a hopeful beginning for this dialogue. When a woman considers a man a "brother," when a man considers a woman a "sister," they are saying that that person is someone with whom they can share and communicate. The very idea of men and women seeing each other as companions and equals brings hope to our lives. Brothers and sisters may experience problems, but they can work on them together, side by side.

My first ten years or so of analysis convinced me that I must write about the brother-sister connection. I often felt as though I were a living example of this uncharted territory of the psyche, always struggling to find a way to converse with this peculiar brother-sister dynamic in myself. In Jungian literature, the relationship was often alluded to—for me, in a tantalizing manner—but with no practical and concrete follow-through. The master himself, Jung, spoke of brother and sister in mythological and alchemical[1] terms, but he never took that next step of bringing them into the arena of individual psychology. Complexes form out of our experiences of archetypal patterns;[2] and, personally, I have seen brother- and sister-complexes (of opposite sex *and* same sex siblings) operating with great autonomy and power in my clients. I believe that analysts have worked with these experiences of clients without a map, so to speak. As my analysts did, we just "wing it," following the dream images and experiences of the individual, with a sense that there is something more to this sibling bond, perhaps even wishing that someone would write about it.

I am convinced that the brother-sister relationship is not only psychologically alive for many individuals, but that it also provides us with hope for our world. Brother and sister point the way toward a new understanding of companionship and mutuality because, first and foremost, they *are* companions. The coming together of opposites[3] in companionship is an experience of profound meaning. This is a power that unites us to ourselves and to others; it is a creative and life-generating force. At this point in history, we *must* remember that there is power, not only in conflict and discord, but also in harmony and equanimity.

---

[1] Alchemy, as an ancient and medieval science, was an attempt to transform base substances often into gold by combining and heating them. Jung saw this transformation process as a metaphor for individuation—the process of becoming a psychologically whole individual through consciously integrating the unconscious.

[2] A complex expresses the pattern in the individual's way of experiencing a particular archetype or cluster of archetypes. It is emotionally charged, and can enhance or limit consciousness. The archetype is a universally experienced psychological phenomenon.

[3] "Opposites" in the psychological sense can refer to opposing tendencies within one individual—masculine and feminine or shadow and ego—or to members of the opposite sex, opposing views or opposing cultures. Jung often spoke of the "tension of the opposites," that friction which must exist for psychological growth to occur.

With a strong sense of purpose, I began this book about the brother-sister relationship and in 1996 had almost completed it. Then a family crisis threw me off balance. I did my work, attended to the family as best I could, and the book was put aside. Years went by. In the spring of 2005, another family crisis occurred, and in my attempts to understand it, I came face to face with the brother-sister relationship in my life again. I took out the book and completed it.

The brother-sister relationship is what gave birth to this book, and it is what drove me back to finish it. I was concerned that I might look at my earlier writing and feel either uninspired or disconnected. Neither occurred—I was ready with the unwritten pages, as though they had been writing themselves inside me all those years. I had come full circle.

I have been asked who I imagine my readers to be—is the book only for women and men who have been close to a brother or sister, or will an only child or same sex siblings find themselves in these pages as well? Let me say that we are all sisters and brothers. And this book is for all of us—for the sisters and brothers who want to explore this dimension of their lives more fully, whether their experiences of the sibling have been creative or destructive, as well as for individuals who aren't even sure that they understand what brother or sister energy is or if they have ever experienced it. I expect that everyone will find pieces of his or her life somewhere in these pages ... because (yes, I know I'm repeating myself) we are all sisters and brothers.

This book is for you, my brothers and sisters. I hope you enjoy reading it as much as I enjoyed writing it.

PART ONE

The Power of Companionship

CHAPTER ONE

Brothers and Sisters as Companions

L isten carefully, and you will hear powerful brother-sister stories more often than you ever imagined.

Janice came in to see me, having learned a little about dream interpretation and eager to learn more. She had recently had multiple dreams about stags, and in her waking life a rare bird had taken up residence in her yard. She knew that these were powerful messages, but she was uncertain what to do with them. As we talked about these images and experiences, two themes emerged. One was the simple idea that her attention was required; she must attend closely to the beings who were showing up at her psychological doorstep. The other, equally simple, was that she must employ care and nurturing when engaging with them.

In Janice's dreams, the stags appeared in her driveway and in her yard. These majestic and powerful beasts were in danger, and it was she to whom they had come for help. From my work with images, I knew that stags are often associated with the brother. However, this is certainly not their only connection, and so far Janice had mentioned nothing about brothers. Then she spoke of the bird now living in her yard and described her love of birding to me. She said that her brother, who had died four years earlier, was also a birder. They had been "soul mates," and she had grieved this loss deeply. Her brother was perhaps the only male in her life who had seen her as an equal and treated her with love and respect.

Janice had grieved for her actual brother, and now the inner brother, as represented by the stags and the rare bird, was calling to her. It was time to attend to him, care for him, and begin to learn about this inner dimension of the brother that had previously been experienced externally in her actual brother. Such imagery as appeared to Janice comes from the collective unconscious, that realm of the psyche that is universal to all human experience and is the source of archetypal energy. Without knowing it, she had begun developing that strength of character and self-worth that a relationship to the archetypal brother can provide; now the development must become a conscious process.

Another client, Martha, had worked in analysis with me for several years. In that time, she had developed an awareness of her overpowering negative brother-complex, stemming from the influence of a brother who had bullied her and forced her into sexually compromising situations repeatedly in her childhood. Our work had included a long, dark struggle with overwhelming self-doubt, which this complex had instilled in her. Martha's ability to keep herself from being pulled into the vortex of the complex had increased considerably. She had come to see herself as valuable, as living in her own life story instead of being an object in others' lives.

Now Martha was on the brink of a new undertaking in her outer life, one that she had been anticipating for some time. As often happens in these situations, all of her negative complexes were activated, and she was struggling to keep a positive attitude and belief in herself. Then she had the following dream:

> *I am having twins, and I also am a twin. All of us are male and female; the twins are always one male and one female. We always have sex with each other, to produce more twins. The sexual relationship begins in the womb and then continues outside. As this becomes socially unacceptable, tubes and tunnels are dug underground. We will have to hide, keep it secret. I am living through generations of twinship.*

This dream asserts that, after many years of working through her dark and destructive brother-complex, it was time for Martha to recognize something altogether different—the archetypal dimension of the brother-sister pair.[1] This dream could have been devastating to Martha at an earlier point in her life, because it presents a positive image of sexual intimacy between brother and sister—an experience

---

[1] The Egyptian brother-sister deities, Isis and Osiris, beginning their conjugal relationship in the womb, come to mind.

that had in childhood been so painful for her. However, after having worked analytically with her own unconscious psyche for a number of years, she was now ready to see the deep and ultimately positive level of union with the inner brother that the dream called her to. Martha's new undertaking in outer life required a connection with the Self, the true center of her personality, and now the dream's symbolic language revealed a profound truth to her: The inner union of brother and sister is an experience of the Self, and as such it centers, deepens, and energizes our psychic life.

As we begin to think in terms of examining the brother-sister relationship, certain questions arise. Is the "relationship" a psychological reality, even when an individual has no siblings? We all have mother and father complexes, even if there has been no known relationship to a parent, because mother and father are patterns of experience that are universal to all humans—that is, they are archetypal images. For example, we often see maternal and paternal instincts[2] emerging spontaneously in young children, whether or not they have had early access to those actual figures in their lives—comforting a doll who has an "owie" or disciplining their stuffed animals. Is the same true for the brother-sister experience? Can we have brother- or sister-complexes even though we don't have biological siblings? How does the brother-sister pattern of relationship in the outer world impact our internal development, if it is negative? positive? overdeveloped? unable to develop?

Having once thought this brother-sister phenomenon might be significant only to individuals who have, like myself, experienced an early bond with their opposite-sex sibling, I finally came to recognize that the inner image of brother-sister union is, in fact, a fundamental pattern that underlies human existence and experience. Images of the relationship in its variety and complexity abound in cultures throughout the world. Stories about brothers and sisters, whether from real life or fairy tales, beckon us to look more closely at the brother-sister connection in the psyche. Clients who have never known a sibling relationship can suddenly dream of having a brother or sister. People like Martha, whose relationship with a brother or sister has been hostile or abusive, may have a powerful experience that pulls them into awareness of a larger dimension to the internal brother-

---

[2] Instinct is the behavioral expression of the psychological pattern of the archetype.

sister pair, like the common dream in which we discover that there are more rooms in our house than we knew of. In archetypal stories, one expression of the brother-sister relationship may restrict, rather than enhance, the individual development of the brother or sister (or both), while another provides an image of support and companionship. We must not shrink away from the pain that comes with such contradictions—lessons of pain are part of our personal and archetypal existence. The many and varied stories give us models to learn from, information about what can be strong, or what can go wrong, in this part of our psyches. These experiences and images feel compelling; they beg to be understood.

The approach that I find most helpful in interpreting fairy tales, dreams, and life experiences is decidedly Jungian. By this I mean a symbolic approach, with the purpose of the investigation being to uncover the psychological *meaning* of the phenomenon, as opposed to its "cause" or even the pathology involved in its expression. As most Jungians will attest, the causes and pathologies are always discovered and worked with along the way, when we are investigating psychological meaning, but if we stop there the individuation process remains unconscious. Individuation, or the conscious recognition, integration, and transformation of unconscious life, is the goal of our human existence, and I believe it must be the major purpose behind any psychological engagement with the brother-sister dynamic. In a Jungian interpretation, we examine every image in a dream or fairy tale as an aspect of the psyche. Even the most negative sister or brother figure is an aspect of the archetypal image of brother-sister union— understanding the negative complex ultimately leads us to understand the potential that lies within us.

Interestingly enough, there is hardly any form the relationship can take that hasn't been given attention in the numerous brother-sister fairy tales that are at our disposal. We see destructive brothers or sisters, overly dependent siblings, both physical and psychological incest, external threats to the sibling relationship, and the brother and sister working together as companions against all odds. Fairy tales also show us the brother-sister archetype in its purest form—the form least affected by individual or cultural overlays. For these reasons, I prefer to focus on fairy tales as a primary source of information about the human experiences of brother and sister.

However, there is an indisputable value in interweaving the concrete and imaginal levels just as they are interwoven in life. Therefore, while I will let fairy tales function as a guide to our deeper understanding of brothers and sisters, I will frequently explore the brother-sister pair in actual concrete relationships, in dreams and fantasies, and in fairy tales in an interchangeable fashion. The archetype exists as a powerful energy in the unconscious, and it is experienced as a living presence in the objective world as well. To isolate one from the other is to create an inhuman boundary, which would not be helpful to anyone striving to understand what the brother-sister dynamic means in his or her life. Similarly, the inner and outer experiences of "brother" and "sister" may often interweave in an individual's life. As we develop psychological awareness, we increase our ability to relate to the internal dimension. In other words, a sister will incorporate into her own personality qualities that she previously saw in her brother, and vice versa.

An important part of Jungian theory is the concept that we all have masculine *and* feminine characteristics in our psyche. These terms may conjure up the simple idea of a man and a woman, but they are far more complicated than they appear. They are symbolic concepts, and can be compared to the ancient Chinese concepts of *Yang* and *Yin*, which encompass the complementary energies of: (yang) light, heat, out-going, driven, moving, initiating, arousing, separating, heaven, spirit; and (yin) dark, cool, in-going, receptive, containing, gestating, enclosing, connecting, nature, earth. Jung believed that all psychological process, and particularly transformation, is based on the relationship between these "opposites." As psychological energies they are complementary, attracting each other and also paradoxically resisting each other. Out in the world, the attraction might be expressed in the saying "opposites attract," while the resistance can be seen in polarizations such as racial tension, gender bias, and war. *Yang* and *Yin* are the two energies of life, and out of their relationship our consciousness is born. Often we experience them as images of a male and a female—mother and father, husband and wife, brother and sister—although each "pair" can ultimately be seen as an internal experience in one individual psyche.

Jung developed a psychological theory which recognized the complex and intricate interplay of these characteristics or energies.

He even spoke of the brother-sister pair as representing an archetypal energy "standing allegorically for the whole concept of opposites."[3] The concept of opposites, and the tension or harmony between them, is of central importance in a psychology that takes the unconscious into account because the conscious and unconscious psychological forces are those opposites in a state of continual motion between union and opposition. Particularly in his extensive work with alchemical texts, Jung speaks of the brother-sister pair as having an archetypal, or universally experienced, level of meaning.[4] His focus is on inner process and the individual's interior experience of this brother-sister archetype.

My work explores the psychological dimensions of the brother-sister relationship as it manifests and develops internally for both women and men. Often when I speak of a woman's development, the particular experience may be one that resonates with men as well, and the same is true for what I refer to as a man's development. In terms of female development, I have come to see the inner brother as an important aspect of the animus for women (the masculine part of her own psyche); by his very nature, the inner brother is *potentially* more accessible, less dangerous or risky to relate to than most other forms of animus energy.

Likewise, for men an inner sister represents the anima (the feminine part of a man's psyche) in her most companionable aspect. In adolescence, young people in the midst of their first quest for romance often find themselves drawn also to other non-romantic kinds of companions of the opposite sex who fill the brother or sister role: they can bare their souls and share things with these "buddies" that they feel less comfortable sharing with a lover because this relationship is safer. A question this tendency may raise is, "To what aspect of ourselves, psychologically, does this experience point?" That question is central to my work.

In the course of looking at this question, we encounter many stories in which the brother or sister is dishonest or dangerous. In these stories, we must open ourselves to an exploration of the shadow,[5] or

---

[3] *CW* 12 § 436.
[4] *CW* 12-14, 16.
[5] Shadow is a psychological term of high importance in Jungian thought, and has become practically a household word. For the purposes of this book, it will be referred to when I speak of the more unknown and unacceptable side of the personality; at times

the dark side of the brother-sister union. All archetypes are images of wholeness, containing both a light and dark nature. Likewise, all positive life experiences and good relationships have their dark and shadowy side, which we come to understand if we stay with the experience long enough.

The brother-sister image conjures up many deep and contradictory feelings, just as do other archetypal figures, such as Mother and Father. The nature of the contradictions is specific to the nature of the archetype. The brother-sister pair has a central meaning—one which can be expressed in relatively simple terms. In a broad sense, by comparison to the father, the brother is a more accessible figure to his sister because of his proximity to her in areas such as psychological, sexual, and physical maturity, shared interests, peers, and abilities. He is less dangerous and risky in that he does not belong to the adult world of responsibility, toil, and troubles. He teaches a woman something that father cannot about her own ability to be with, but not controlled by, a male figure. Sister, meanwhile, holds none of the ominous and sometimes ubiquitous power that mother has for a man. She meets him on his own terms. Theirs is a relationship of equality.

Related to other figures of the opposite sex, because they are family brother and sister are more accessible to one another, for good or ill, and do not call each other into the frightening "exogamous"[6] experience. For this same reason, they are less risky figures to each other than is the lover. Brother may challenge and engage his sister in spirited activity, but he is her genetic and psychological "enantiomorph," like and unlike her at the same time.

The brother is best and most succinctly defined as the archetypal image of the "male companion" or the "companion-as-other." With him as a consciously known component in her psyche, a woman can forge a "new world." Likewise, sister is the female companion for a man. Witness the historical or cultural situations in which men and women begin to refer to each other as brother and sister. These are times when pioneering and creating a new way are the foremost goals. The authority and protection which the brother offers are at the sister's

I will refer to a deeper more archetypal dimension of the shadow (as in the above reference), which touches on the dark side of the human experience.

    [6] The terms "exogamous" and "endogamous" will be used occasionally in this text. "Exogamous" refers to a relationship outside the family circle, and "endogamous" refers to familial relationships.

own level, and vice versa. They are "in this together." Because of this mutuality, a strong positive brother-sister relationship gives both parties *faith in their own lives*.

On the strictly biological level, the brother and sister as siblings are genetically more "kin" to each other than any other relative combinations are. They can provide for each other an image of "what I would be if I were a boy (girl)." This brings to mind the paradox inherent in the relationship: opposition and similarity exist side by side, irreconcilable yet reconciled.

On the archetypal level, the equality of brother and sister is clearly present in the mythological brother-sister pair, Apollo and Artemis.[7] As personifications of the sun (Apollo) and the moon (Artemis), they function in harmony, each ruling over an equal domain. In the Olympian hierarchy, Apollo and Artemis are unique as neither is above nor below the other, unlike, for example, the father-king Zeus who rules over all the other gods and goddesses.

However, in outer life, brother-sister relationships often are not equal and harmonious. (Similarly, actual mothers and fathers seldom "live up to" the archetypal ideals of absolute authority and protection placed on them by their children.) It is the inner brother-sister image—the archetype—that contains the notion of equality as a psychic potential. We humans are ill equipped to relate to archetypal energy in its fullness, though we may long to. The actual relationship between the siblings only awakens the archetype within us, and this awakening is the beginning of the long journey toward individuation and true intrapsychic companionship.

There are men and women whose early experiences with mother or father give them a strong and positive relation to their own contrasexual natures. When the positive relation comes from brother or sister (or from other sources of that energy), there is an essential difference. The individual with a positive brother- or sister-complex has a feeling of operating *with*, or alongside, this "other" as opposed to operating *for* it. Sometimes this is a subtle distinction, but it can also be extreme. Picture a woman who shares ideas, duties, and skills with her (male) co-workers versus a woman who seeks to uphold the status quo, enforce existing rules, and please those in charge. This

---

[7] See my notes on Schmidt, Selected Annotated Bibliography, p. 201. Schmidt uses the Apollo-Artemis image as a model for more equality in the marital relationship.

reflects the stark difference between seeing "masculine" energy (here projected onto men or the culture) as father versus seeing it as brother.

The reality of what a young child experiences in the brother-sister realm, be it through a personal brother or sister, or another "brothering" or "sistering" figure during the early years, is the most important *external* factor in how the inner brother/sister will develop. The relationship can be difficult; the sibling may be cruel, hostile, or aggressive. Some brothers and sisters find that they have very little in common, or that they are in competition for parental favors rather than forming a more direct relationship with each other.

In these cases, a "negative" complex forms around brother or sister energy. The complex then obscures the potential that is so important in the archetype, something that is true of any powerful complex. For example, a woman with a negative brother-complex may have great difficulty relating to men of her generation in a straightforward and companionable manner, always projecting onto them the brother-persecutor or the betrayer-of-trust. This kind of complex negates the potential within the archetypal brother-sister pair in which the brother or sister companion can be trusted with secrets. Or a man with a negative sister-complex may find himself feeling fiercely competitive with women, angry when he thinks "they" get special attention, as though he is once again vying with his sisters for parental favor.

These relationship patterns ultimately point to difficulties in one's sense of connectedness and companionship between the inner brother and sister. The "hostility" between these inner archetypal figures outweighs their potential for a "loving" companionship. The individual with such inner conflict will manifest it in various ways. For example, the woman described above may "keep herself down" in a stalemate of indecision or smoldering self-resentment, and have a difficult time getting out of the bind that polarization creates. It is the inner brother-persecutor, not so much the outer, who punishes her and creates this block. Likewise, the angry man may have become a "black-and-white thinker"—"it's her or me"—rejecting his internal feeling nature. He needs to fight constantly to prove that he is more worthy than his "sisters" because he does not believe it himself. At a very deep level, they both have difficulty experiencing the faith in their own lives that a strong sense of inner brother-sister union brings.

We must work through the experiences that hold us in a poor attitude toward our own inner brother or sister before the potential of this inner quality can be recognized. The complex may be negative, as in the examples above, or positive, as described earlier. In either case, a transformation process must occur in order to free up the internal energy from the complex. It is as though we all carry within us this treasure, yet so few people really know it. The treasure is the brother-sister archetype, and its potential can be seen in countless stories that have come down to us through the ages, the brother-sister fairy tales.

CHAPTER TWO

Bonding-Wounding-Healing/ Redemption

THE PATTERN OF TRANSFORMATION

In this book, I map out the course of psychic development that can occur for sisters and brothers, a development that enriches and expands our ability to be in the world as companions. As we explore the brother-sister archetype, we begin to recognize the transformation of the relationship from the concrete experience of an early bond between the siblings to the development of the brother-sister relationship as a known inner psychic reality. I see this transformation occurring over and over again, no matter how many turns the relationship may take on inner or outer levels that temporarily abort the transformation. I will elaborate on the patterns of some of these turns in the course of this book, but always with an eye on the potential transformation inherent in our human experience of the brother-sister pair.

The transformation process in the brother-sister relationship occurs in three simple stages that form a pattern that exists *a priori* (before consciousness) in the psyche: bonding, wounding, and healing/redemption.

BONDING

The first stage is "bonding." In it, the brother and sister function as a unit. Psychologically, they are bound to one another in a symbiotic experience which is powerful but of limited duration. The bonding phase is an "innocent" phase in which an identification exists between the brother and sister that serves to make them "feel whole." In Jungian terms, the brother and sister in this phase are in an state of "*participation mystique*," an unconscious state of identification with another.[1] This is a natural psychic condition in primitives and in children, and it is a powerful aspect of the sibling relationship for a brother's sister or a sister's brother,[2] individuals for whom the brother-sister archetype is central.

In speaking of *participation mystique*, Jung says:

> When I and another person have an unconscious relation to the same *important fact*, I become in part identical with him, and because of this I orient myself to him as I would to the complex in question were I conscious of it.[3] (Italics mine.)

The brother-sister relationship is a carrier of the Self, that "important fact," the archetypal experience of union or wholeness, which is the center of the whole personality. The specific form of union represented by the brother-sister image is relational, companionable, and loving. It brings together "hostile opposites" in a creative and loving way.[4] The "young" brother and sister have an unconscious connection to the Self which they project onto one another. For example, as children they may experience such a profound sense of togetherness that they are happiest when they are unencumbered by other relationships. They may create a safe and secluded world for themselves in which only they are welcome. I have known brother-sister pairs whose childhoods are defined by a "we're in this together" spirit of comradeship. They are "soul mates," and the identification so characteristic of *participation mystique* gives a sense of completion and security. This brother-sister dynamic can exist

---

[1] *CW* 13 § 462 and 66. "*Participation mystique*" is a term used by anthropologist Levy-Bruhl and adapted by Jung. As Jung has pointed out, modern humanity is guilty of considering itself above the primitive's experience of *participation mystique* with nature or the cosmos, while shamelessly indulging in projections and prejudices which in themselves indicate an unconscious identification with the object of the projection. This identification is a form of *participation mystique*.

[2] I use these terms throughout the book in reference to individuals for whom the brother-sister archetype is central. For the reader who is familiar with Jungian concepts, my terms may evoke a recollection of the "father's daughter," an epithet that indicates a woman who is bound to the father's values—for her, father energy has a strong psychological pull. The brother's sister and sister's brother are individuals for whom brother-sister energy has a strong psychological pull.

[3] *CW* 10 § 69.

[4] *CW* 16 § 410.

even for individuals who are not actually related. As with any archetypal force, it is a psychological phenomenon that is not bound to the limits of concrete reality.

This kind of bond can also be experienced imaginally when no actual sibling is present. For example, an only child fantasized from early childhood about an older brother who would show up and heroically save her family. This fantasy brother was her image of the hero, a masculine (animus) figure who she said could "lead her to a better place." Hero fantasies, like this one, belong to the age of innocence, but they also allow us little protection.

WOUNDING

When the autonomy of the brother-sister bond is disturbed, the stage of "wounding" begins. It usually occurs when the brother or sister is attracted to another relationship or special interest in the outside world whose call is greater than that of the brother-sister bond. Often, this break occurs when one of the siblings has a first romance. For a young boy or girl who has been in a state of *participation mystique* with an actual or imagined brother/sister figure, this is usually a painful or bittersweet experience.

The experience of wounding signals the beginning of growing up for the sister or brother. He or she is called out into the greater culture, away from the oneness of the sibling bond into differentiation. In the life experiences that follow this initial wound, the woman confronts or is confronted by other masculine energy that is not from the brother, and the man is confronted by feminine energy in its non-sister form(s).

During this time, before a conscious relationship has been established with the inner brother (for the woman) and the inner sister (for the man), the brother or sister may continue to project qualities of this inner companion onto others just as they had done earlier with each other. In other words, they will relate to brother or sister energy externally, seeing it in another person, instead of recognizing these qualities in themselves. This process of projection is probably necessary initially; however, as the brother and sister develop into adulthood, they must recognize and consciously withdraw these projections. When this occurs, a new relationship with the internal brother-sister archetype can be established by each of them, as well as a deeper understanding of the relationship with the outer brother or sister.

For example, with one brother and sister, the close bond that existed between them when they were young was wounded when the brother became involved in his first romance. He appeared to "turn his back" on his sister. The sister experienced the loss of her intimate relationship with her brother as a betrayal, and the brother did betray his own feeling nature (which he had projected onto his sister) for some time. However, later in adulthood, he recognized what his relationship with his sister had meant to him. He could finally look back on those years and see how his early connection with his sister had informed his understanding of relationships, particularly with women.

It is the conscious awareness of the wound that eventually ushers the sibling into his or her individuation process. In another very strong brother-sister bond, the brother was called away on his own path when his sister was still quite young. Her wound was great, and remained almost entirely unconscious until she reached the age that her brother had been when they separated. Then it became clear that her call to individuation was still linked to his, and she had to work through this loss and separation in order to become a healthy young woman.

HEALING/REDEMPTION

Ultimately, and after a long trial, the sister or brother is able to begin healing the wound and reconnecting on an inner level with the other. This "healing/redemption" stage confronts the individual with great challenges. The experiences brought on by the wound move the brother or sister outside the realm of contrasexual energy into a struggle to find personal identity that is rooted in his or her own gender. The process is different for women and men.[5]

For a woman to experience a mature connection to the inner brother-sister image, she must become grounded and centered in her feminine nature. In the course of her psychological development, a feminine ego first separates from and then returns to the domain of Mother. It is her

---

[5] However, each will experience the other's process more indirectly in the anima/animus regions of the psyche.

task to become aware of the dark and light aspects of her feminine nature. Her ability to inhabit that space—to psychologically "mother" her own developing potential and not be held back by her negative mother-complex—determines whether she may finally redeem her "brother," thus making conscious both her experience of inner strength and her ability to relate to men as friends and companions in her outer life. In the healing/redemption stage, the image of brother-sister union becomes an inner experience of creative harmony which allows the woman to move to a higher level of consciousness.

For a man to be in proper relationship to his inner sister, he must struggle with his shadow, the dark side of masculine aggression and power. In fairy tales and dreams, this may appear in the form of father, a dark magician, or a supernatural powermonger, to name only a few possibilities. It is a power that threatens the man's development and seduces him with its "supremacy" in outer life. His internal sister is helpful during this experience, as she has a deeply intuitive connection to the relationship between the material and spiritual worlds. Other men are at a disadvantage in this respect compared to a sister's brother.

The transformation from bonding to redemption is potentially a lifelong process. Psychologically, there is a battle between the tendency toward "incest" or bottled-in, endogamous energy, and the psyche's outward, exogamous movement to connect with the world. The intimate nature of the "bonding" phase may actually result in concrete incest, a too-narrow acting out of bottled-in energy. Yet this phase also contains the seed for its own transformation as it calls us to conscious companionship.

During the healing/redemption phase, the individual will reconnect, this time consciously, with the psychological power and energy that brother/sister symbolizes. In Jungian terms this reconnecting leads to a psychological experience of the *coniunctio*[6] (often portrayed in alchemy as brother-sister union), a consciously sought and experienced union of the opposites that were once bound unconsciously:

---

[6] The *coniunctio* is the consciously sought psychological union of opposites, a difficult union to achieve, yet highly creative and vitalizing. When we are able to experience a coming together of aspects of our own personalities that once were separated and estranged, we grow in self-awareness *and* in our ability to relate to the world around us.

> In this union ... Sol and Luna [Brother and Sister] themselves
> become spirit .... The "coniunctio" ... is by nature never an initial
> state: it is always the product of a process or the goal of endeavor.[7]

Sol and Luna's becoming spirit suggests that these brother-sister figures are now available as intrapsychic components and as aids to the individuation process.

The healing/redemption stage of the brother-sister relationship is a time of great energy. The psychological work of this stage is more obviously rewarding than that of the wounding stage because the experience of wounding is a descent, and the healing/redemption stage provides a movement upward. The healing/redemption stage may enter consciousness with a burst of energy, but it actually is a slow and gradual process, almost imperceptible at times. The healing that occurs in this phase does not take place overnight; rather it is experienced and re-experienced throughout this period. It can be the longest stage of development, sometimes taking the individual through the second half of life into old age.

During a time of major transition in my life, after a long period of wounding, I began to recognize that the "brother" still lived within me, and I had the following dream:

A worldwide catastrophe has occurred, which caused the near-extinction of humanity. Now the survivors are forming tribal groups, and these groups are choosing the regions of the world they will inhabit. There is a long corridor spanning the world, and walking down it one can eventually make contact with all the tribal groups. I am in a group together with some members of my family. My brother has been in the group, but his father brutally abuses him and makes his life miserable. It seems that although I recognize that this figure is likely to be my father too, my life is spared such torment. The father is no threat to me. One day, my brother is missing, and I hear that his father is raging and swearing he will find him. I decide to take a walk down the corridor to find my brother first. I walk for many miles, and far from my group I see some people coming out of a conference room. My brother is one of them, and with him are his wife and young son. They look happy, he hugs his son, they have just "signed on" with this tribe. I go to my brother and tell him how happy I am that he has made this break, how I believe this is the right choice and that his secret is safe with me. I warn him against the father, who is looking for him. Then I bid him farewell, saying that we will meet again.

As the dream suggests, my inner brother had been wounded partly by the negative masculine energy which appears in the dream as the father. Shadowy masculine energy, just as life-denying as shadowy feminine energy, often reveals itself during the psychological growing-up phase of a brother's sister. It can be part of the wounding. In my twenties, I was surprised by this kind of negative masculine energy, sinister and destructive, and the suffering that ensued wounded my uroboric[8] brother-sister bond—and the brother-animus—and forced me to grow up. In other words, my companionable and intellectual way of being in the world and with men was suddenly not enough when I was faced with these dark aspects of the masculine world. I was an adult woman on my own, who couldn't hide behind the brother relationship, and I had to learn some new psychological truths about myself and the world.

For some women who are very attached to their own inner "brother energy," the brother is brutalized during the wounding stage. In my case, the trust that "all men are brothers" led me into pain and despair. My brother-animus was in danger. This kind of brutalization to the brother-animus may be due to the sister's having held on too tightly to the bond, attempting to ward off her inevitable growing up. It may also be because the woman keeps projecting her inner experience of the brother-sister connection "out there" in a world, where it isn't met or understood. It only gets trampled. In my dream, for the brother to be healed, there must be a hiding away and a strengthening of all that he represents.

Jung alludes to this idea when he refers to brother-sister union as a secret not understood by common man—the "prerogative of Kings." Here Jung is speaking of incest, but in the archetypal realm. He refers to the Egyptian Pharaohs' practice of brother-sister marriage as an inner image of wholeness. The conscious realization of this union of opposites "is naturally coupled with the danger of falling victim to the shadow, but the danger also brings with it the possibility of consciously deciding not to become its victim."[9]

----

[8] "Uroboric" is a term that refers to a state of unconscious wholeness, symbolized by the snake in a circle biting its own tail.

[9] *CW* 16 § 418-420.

This "decision" occurs symbolically in my dream, when I, the sister, discover where my brother will be and wish him well. The story of brother and sister will go on, but "for some time" sister will carry the "secret" of her brother's new family and new life, and brother's healing will be taking place away from the rest of the world in the unconscious. The region of the new world where my brother is going with his family is a place in the psyche where he will be safe, and this is a requirement for healing to take place.

CHAPTER THREE

Enchantment

While poring over brother-sister fairy tales, I became aware of a compelling motif arising over and over—that of enchantment. This is a motif common to fairy tales in general, but the frequency of its occurrence in brother-sister tales is striking. Usually the brother is enchanted; sometimes it is both brother and sister. Enchantment plays a major role in a number of the fairy tales I describe later in this book.

Enchantment in fairy tales is a curse or bewitchment which is placed upon one or more characters or upon a place by someone with magical powers. One of the most common forms of enchantment, especially in the brother-sister fairy tales, is transformation from human into animal form. In some other types of enchantment, a character might be cursed so that he or she can no longer speak, or he or she may be required to perform certain tasks—for example, a female might be forced to kill all her suitors. Sometimes, a whole castle or kingdom is enchanted—it might be frozen in time, or everyone in the castle might be put into a state of despair.

There is always a purpose to the enchantment. In the course of the tale, the enchanted person learns some lesson or comes to some new awareness; and, once this is accomplished, the spell is lifted; the individual is "redeemed." In cases of a human-to-animal transformation, von Franz says that the animal form the human takes represents an instinctive, lower level of functioning (lower with regard to cerebral activity, that is). This puts limits on the transformed human's actions, because as instinct, the animal behavior cannot deviate from its inherent pattern.[1] I believe that the limits as well as the focus or lesson that the enchantment brings are important aspects of the entire psychological process of the enchantment. So, even when enchantment comes from a "negative" source, such as a witch or evil sorcerer, it is an expression of the mystery in life, which takes us into the uncharted regions of the unconscious and always results in new psychological insight.

The source of enchantment is often an envious, hostile, or aggressive figure who has special powers. In the brother-sister tales, it may be a witch, an enchantress, a sorcerer, a wizard, an all-powerful father or mother who has dark powers. The source, then, can be masculine or feminine.

When the enchantment comes from one of these dark figures, it is often seen as a "curse"; however, there are notable exceptions, in which the figure casting the enchanting spell is not sinister at all. For example, in Arthurian legend, Merlin uses his animal spells to teach the child Arthur about his own animal, or instinctual, nature.[2] Under Merlin's spell, Arthur becomes a fish or a goose, and in that transformed state he is forced to rely on a different way of being in the world, a way he might otherwise miss. Merlin uses this approach to get Arthur's attention and to teach him lessons that can't be learned from books; these are the natural lessons of the instincts, the non-cognitive parts of our psyche. It sometimes takes a jolt for us to listen to these instinctive voices. What better jolt than being forced into a new body—the context suddenly looks altogether different!

It is significant that brothers and sisters rarely have the good connection to their enchanters that is so evident with Arthur and Merlin. Nevertheless, all enchantment has at its base the kind of lesson that is apparent in the Merlin-Arthur stories. Something *is* out of balance; brother and sister will often need to face a dangerous conflict in order to restore it.

In everyday life, our most common relationship with our instincts is that they get in the way of our desire for conscious control. We are in tension or conflict. This pattern is reflected in fairy tales, and it is suddenly reversed when a spell is cast so that conscious control is out

---

[1] Marie-Louise von Franz, *The Psychological Meaning of Redemption Motifs in Fairytales* (Toronto: Inner City Books, 1980), pp. 7-8, 21.

[2] T. H. White, *The Once and Future King* (New York: Berkley Publishing, 1958).

of the question. For example, a prince who wants to have his own way is turned into a bird so that "having his own way" is no longer a possibility. Now, as an instinctive creature himself, he must learn to live in harmony with the instincts. This tension between desire for conscious control and the unconscious instinctive life must be dealt with; finding a balance is crucial, and the lesson must be learned while the character is in the enchanted animal form. Even if the enchantment comes from an "evil force," to learn its lesson is essential.

The fairy tales are specific about the source of the enchantment as well as the form the enchantment takes so that if we look at each story in terms of its own unique images, these images will lead us to the "problem" posed by the particular enchantment and the particular lesson that must be learned from it. Translated into psychological terms, the enchantment in brother-sister fairy tales often reflects a situation in which a powerful archetypal force has split off from the dominant attitude, and that force is influencing consciousness in a "cloaked" or unconscious manner through enchantment.

Some of these concepts can be seen in a powerful dream about enchantment I had when I was five years old, which strongly resembles a fairy tale:

My family (mother, father, brother, me) is together, driving across an old swaying bridge. We are in a very cavernous, desert-like region, and the bridge is across a deep ravine. We know that we are going to a new village on the other side. We get there, and we are standing in a market square. Everything is foreign and strange. People wear long robes. A strange man comes up to us, he looks like a magician. He throws feathers in my path, as well as those of my brother and my father. We are curious about what this means. People shy away from us. Someone says, "Don't you know? You will be swans before nightfall." I look at my mother, and she seems to recede. Then it is only my brother and I; we have left the village and are walking down a dirt road. We know we must stay outside of the town. We have grown wings and feathers.

We are sort of searching for our father, and sort of just wandering. As we walk, we learn more about our situation. There is a wizard who hunts swans; he is evil and must be avoided. We sleep along the road in secluded areas, and keep wandering. One day, we see the wizard coming across a field with a troop of followers. They are coming for us. We stand, feeling helpless. A voice tells us that we can use our wings to fly away from him. Suddenly, we are airborne, and we fly way up to the clouds. We see our father there, and there are lots of other swans and birds around. It's like a community. The clouds are billowy, and we feel safe.

In my dream, both my brother and I are enchanted—turned into swans—by a strange male magician, and then later pursued by another sinister male wizard. The magician and wizard represent a negative archetypal force from the masculine world, split off from my consciousness, that threatened to enchant my young life. Perhaps if I had had a better connection to this "magic" energy from the masculine realm that the magician/wizard represented, the lesson would have gone easier, but for various reasons, some of which I learned only much later, I didn't. My relation to the masculine realm was influenced by my father, who had spent World War II in a foreign prison camp, where he was brutally tortured. Because he had no way of processing or communicating these experiences, they remained unconscious, hidden deep within his shadow as an ominous persecutor/aggressor, though outwardly he remained a gentle and kind father. This persecutor/aggressor energy was transmitted to me via the unconscious, as unconscious contents always move between parents and child. In the dream, the magician and wizard influence my brother and me through means that are unfathomable (unconscious) to me—they take on the energy of the ominous male persecutor.

My relationship with the masculine side of life was also influenced by my relationship with my brother with whom I had a strong connection. This relationship activated the brother "imago" in my unconscious. In order to maintain my own individuality and my inner brother-connection, "we" both had to become conscious of the repressive energy represented by the magician/wizard. This lesson comprised much of my first-half-of-life journey, and my dream told me that in that journey I had to learn what it means to be a swan.

The swan's life is characterized by transformation. It is a bird that goes from "ugly-duckling" awkwardness at birth to the essence of beauty and grace in adulthood.[3] The capacity for this type of life cycle is indicated by the swan image. My brother and I had become swans

---

[3] Our father was a swan too (also susceptible to the "male magic"), but he was not on our journey, though he did reconnect with us at the end of it.

and would need to learn together. Our task was a risky business, since the evil wizard, likely in partnership with the original sorcerer, was pursuing us and wanted to destroy our spirit. These sinister figures were symbols of the "male magic" of which I was unconscious. The enchantment had put my "brother" and me right in the middle of a psychological struggle with my "blind spot." I came to understand something of that blind spot decades later, but it was already foreshadowed in my dream as a five-year-old.

So, when enchantment occurs, a new and unknown way replaces the present way of being. The new mode is where the lessons are learned. The fact that the enchantment is experienced as a *problem* means that the archetypal power that brought about the enchantment must somehow be pulled back into a balanced relationship to the whole personality so that it stops doing its "dirty work" from the outside, and the enchanted state can end. In everyday life, someone who has felt persecuted by others begins to wake up to her own self-loathing. Now she can start to *really* care about herself and speak up for herself in a new way.

In the bonding stage, enchantment serves a dual purpose. First, it reinforces the bond between brother and sister. If one or both are transformed into animals, for example, they may become even closer, needing each other more than ever to survive. But at the same time, enchantment imposes new conditions on that bond, and those conditions eventually lead to a new level of self-knowledge and a development beyond the bonded state.

In both outer life and fairy tales, enchantment weaves in and out of the "bonding" and "wounding" stages of the brother-sister relationship. At times, a stage may be so dominated by enchantment that it seems as if the stage itself *were* the enchantment. This is the illusion of enchantment, part of its universal power. It threatens to "take over" our psychological process from time to time, sometimes successfully.

As this work unfolds, the potential for transformation contained in the "curse" of enchantment will become as clear as the pain it also inflicts. This pain must be experienced, but with transformation as its ultimate goal.

PART TWO

The Sister's Work

CHAPTER FOUR

The Story: "Brother and Sister"

In Part Two, I will explore a woman's psychological development with regard to the transformation of the brother-sister relationship. Because it is an archetypal experience, this psychological development can occur for any woman, although it may be most evident in women who have had a brother-type relationship early in life. (Indeed, even men may recognize themselves in these pages.) The pattern of transformation moves from the state of bonding to wounding and, finally, to healing of the wound and redemption of the experience of psychological unity imaged in the inner brother-sister pair. To illustrate this process I will use the Grimms' tale "Brother and Sister" primarily, but will also include examples from contemporary life and from other fairy tales and archetypal stories to amplify the material.

* * * * *

"Brother and Sister"

Little Brother took his sister by the hand and said: "Since our mother died we have had no happiness. Our stepmother beats us and treats the dog better than us. God pity us. Come, we will go forth together into the wide world."

They walked the whole day, and when it rained the little sister said: "Heaven and our hearts are weeping together." They came to a forest by evening and slept in a hollow tree. The next day they awoke in the sun's heat and the brother said he was so thirsty he must find a brook from which to drink. He took sister by the hand and went to find one. But the wicked stepmother was a witch, and she had crept after them and bewitched all the brooks in the forest.

At the first brook, sister heard it say: "Who drinks of me will be a tiger," and she begged her brother not to drink from it, for fear that he would tear her to pieces. The brother agreed to wait, though he was very thirsty.

At the second brook, sister heard it say: "Who drinks of me will be a wolf," and again she begged her brother not to drink, for fear that he would devour her. The brother again agreed, but said he must drink the next time.

At the third brook, sister heard: "Who drinks of me will be a roebuck," and she begged her brother not to drink, saying, "You will become a roebuck and run away from me." But it was too late, and the brother was a young roebuck.

They wept, and the sister said, "I will never, never leave you." She gave her golden garter for his collar and wove a leash from rushes, and then they walked deeper and deeper into the woods.

They found a little house where they lived in the woods, and were happy for some time. The roe played around her, and at night she used his back for a pillow.

One day the King of that country held a great hunt in the forest. Hearing the blasts of the horns, the barking of the dogs, and the merry shouts of the huntsmen, the roebuck was anxious to be out, and finally sister let him go. She said "I must shut my door for fear of the rough huntsmen, so this evening knock and say 'my little sister, let me in.'" The roebuck ran away, happy in the open air.

The King and huntsmen saw him, tried and failed to catch him. The next day, when the hunt began again, the roebuck again had no peace, jumping about and saying, "I must be off." This day a huntsman wounded him a little in the foot, so he limped. A hunter crept after him to the cottage and heard his password, then went back and told the King what he had seen and heard.

The sister was frightened when she saw her roe hurt; she washed and dressed the wound with herbs and sent him to bed to heal. But the wound was so slight that he felt well the next morning, and was again ready for the hunt. The sister cried, saying he would be killed and she would be alone and forsaken by the world. He pleaded saying, "I feel as if I must jump out of my skin when I hear the bugle horns." She finally relented. She had a heavy heart, but he bounded with joy and health.

The King allowed the roe to be hunted all day long, then went himself to the cottage at nightfall. He spoke the words "dear little sister, let me in," and walked in to see a beautiful maiden. Then he asked her to marry him, and she said yes if she could take the roe. The King agreed and she tied her roe with the cord of rushes and took it in her hand and followed the King away from the cottage.

She became the Queen and lived happily for some time. The roebuck was tended and cherished and ran happily in the palace gardens. But the wicked stepmother, who had thought they had died miserably, heard of their happiness, and jealousy rose in her heart and gave her no peace. She had an ugly daughter with only one eye, who was also jealous. The woman waited for the opportunity to bring them to misfortune again.

After a time, the Queen gave birth to a baby boy, and the King was away hunting; so the old witch took the form of the chambermaid, and took the Queen to her bath. She had made it so hot that soon the young Queen was suffocated, and then she put her daughter in the Queen's bed. She gave her the shape and look of the Queen, but she could not make good the lost eye, so the girl lay on that side.

When the King came home, he was glad to hear that he had a son, but the old woman would not let him see his wife, saying that she must have rest. But at midnight, the nurse who was sitting by the cradle saw the true Queen come in. She took the baby and nursed it, then went to the corner where the roe lay and stroked its back. Then she went silently away. The next morning she asked the guards whether anyone had entered the palace in the night, and they said no.

This happened many nights, and the Queen never spoke. The nurse always saw, but she did not dare to tell anyone. After some time, the Queen began to speak. She said: "How fares my child, how fares my roe? Twice shall I come, then never more." The nurse went to the King and told him of this. The next evening he went into the nursery to watch by the child, and at midnight the Queen again appeared and said: "How fares my child, how fares my roe? Once will I come, then never more." She nursed the baby and left. The King dared not speak, but came again the next night. She said: "How fares my child, how fares my roe? This time I come, then never more." The King could not stop himself from springing towards her and saying, "You can be none other than my dear wife." She said, "Yes, I am your dear wife," and at that moment she gained life again.

Then she told the King all, and he led the old woman and her daughter before the judge. The judgment was delivered, and the daughter was taken into the forest where she was torn to pieces by wild beasts, but the witch was cast into the fire and burnt. As soon as she was burnt to ashes, the roebuck received his human form again, so the sister and brother lived happily together all their lives.[1]

* * * * *

---

[1] Brothers Grimm, No. 11, pp. 67-73.

Just from the title, "Brother and Sister," it's obvious that the theme of this fairy tale is the brother-sister relationship. Their strong connection provides a feeling of family and belonging as they wander away from their physical home, deep into the forest. The young sister-heroine thrives as she grows up in the forest with her enchanted roebuck-brother companion. They share authority, and they complement each other. The sister consistently provides grounding and connection to nature, and the brother is consistently active, exhibiting "going out" energy. Sometimes it may seem that one kind of energy is more needed than the other, or that one is "right" for the situation and the other "wrong." However, no sooner do we start to form such an opinion than the tables turn, and we recognize the balancing effect the brother and sister have on each other.

The greatest obstacle to the pair in this tale is their stepmother, who reveals to us the dark side of the archetypal Great Mother, insinuating her influence by means of enchantment and seeking control over the children. In the beginning of the story, the sister leaves the stepmother at her brother's behest, only to realize much later that she must find a way to re-connect with the mother archetype in order to develop into womanhood.

CHAPTER FIVE

Bonding

1. BROTHER AND SISTER, AND THE WITCH

At the beginning of this fairy tale, the sister and brother live with their inhospitable stepmother; they apparently have no parents in whom they can trust—mother dead, father unmentioned. Their relationship with each other is the primary relationship for both siblings. The brother takes the initiative in changing their situation, takes the sister by the hand, and leads her away. Symbolically, these two are bonded, partners in the journey of life, going forth together into the world.

Their bondedness is reflected in the way the brother relates their story. He speaks of "their" treatment by the stepmother in this manner: "*we* have had no happiness ... she beats *us* ... if *we* come near she kicks *us* ... *our* meals are the hard crusts." It is as though there is no separate identity for the two. They exist as a pair. Psychologically, this depicts a state of undifferentiated bonding of the psychic elements "brother" and "sister" within an individual. We will typically first experience this state outwardly in an actual relationship between brother and sister, or perhaps between unrelated buddies, who are inseparable.[1]

At the outset of the tale, the brother figure, the male companion for the young female, is an aspect of positive masculine and outgoing

---

[1] For example, in the movie, *Riding in Cars With Boys* (2001), directed by Penny Marshall, we see this sort of inseparable relationship forming between the son and daughter of two teenage best friends. The best friends are fifteen-year-old girls who both got pregnant accidentally. They are too immature to parent their children, but the children have each other, and they provide "family" for each other where it otherwise does not exist.

energy. This kind of energy is needed in order to get the pair out of their restrictive environment, one in which they are tormented and treated "worse than the dog" by their stepmother. The brother-sister pair must, albeit temporarily, separate from the powerful negative mother figure to survive. This separation is necessary not just for the survival of the brother and sister in the external world but also for the inner brother-sister relationship. It is particularly important for the sister's own individual psychological development, which will be thwarted if she continues to live in this "place" where she is under the power of the dark negative mother. It is both an internal psychological space, where the girl has self-doubt and self-loathing, and an externally stifling environment.

An example of this same kind of situation can be seen in a client of mine whose father committed suicide when she was in early adolescence. He was a brilliant man whose emotional life had been deteriorating since her earliest memory. She was left with her mother, who was emotionally immature, and an older brother. Her mother was depressed and pessimistic about life. She was unable to help her children through the tragedy. Instead, she sought solace elsewhere, and spoke only in terms of how her husband's suicide had ruined *her* life. The children were on their own, in a sense. At the time of their father's death, the girl's brother promised to take care of her always; he said, "you don't need to worry, *we'll* be all right." From that time until her adulthood, this woman's brother was her "hero." He was her way out of the repressive environment of her mother's world.

When the male companion takes a heroic position, he ultimately inspires his sister to have faith in her own life. However, the "hero" *and* the bond may be projected onto the external person, as they were in this woman's adolescence. The brother/hero becomes the carrier of the girl's sense of unity or wholeness. While the "hero" is an essential figure to help the young girl out of the negative atmosphere, she must eventually connect with this heroic nature, and her own sense of wholeness, internally.

A girl or woman becomes a participant in a brother-sister bond when her external experience of brother—the actual person—activates the "companion-as-other" archetype within her psyche. In this stage, the brother is often a positive animus figure, providing a good connection to the masculine realm. Jung says a woman's animus is always first "awakened" by an external relationship with a male,[2] and the brother-animus is no exception. As with any unconscious contents, the animus is projected, and there is always a risk that the sister will fail to withdraw the projection, thus allowing the outside masculine figures to live her animus for her. Whether a fantasy brother figure, the brothering figures in her surroundings, or an actual brother in the girl's life, "brother" is likely to have this strong external pull.

When the brother brings his sister an experience of togetherness and oneness, as in the tale and the woman's story related above, this is a "Self experience" for the woman. The specific Self-image here is one of relationship—the image of the brother-sister pair—and, for a brother's sister or a sister's brother, *relationship is a numinous experience.* In strong brother-sister relationships, the siblings will invariably have these Self-experiences *with* each other.

The struggle of the brother and sister to make a place for themselves is often expressed as a struggle against a destructive parental force. If the strength of the brother-sister pair in "Brother and Sister" is to become a consciously known inner experience for the young woman, it must fight its way past a powerful will to destroy, which is symbolized by the stepmother.

We must all fight against our own self-destructive tendencies, and these tendencies often feel as though they have always been there and were there even before we came into being. In fact, they were! Self-destructive tendencies are passed on unconsciously from parent to child (and even from the parent-culture to individuals). This is one reason why they so frequently show up in fairy tales as a parent-figure, such as the stepmother in "Brother and Sister." Each individual must break beyond the limits put on him by his predecessors, and the brother and sister experience these limits as a will to destroy their union. In terms of concrete life experience, the dark negative mother of this tale could point to an early experience of the actual mother—some non-nurturing tendency in a girl's mother, which feels dangerous to her. With such a mother in our lives, the inner mother imago becomes imbued with negative energy. An example of this would be the previously-mentioned woman's depressed mother (p. 38), who was unable to nurture and protect her children through the tragic loss of

---

[2] *CW* 9ii § 42.

their father. The mother's negative energy is internalized by the girl, and just as the stepmother shows up later in the tale, "she" may be experienced by the woman later in her life under the guise of depression, suicidal thoughts, addiction, a feeling of self-abnegation, or externally as unhealthy and destructive situations that threaten to rob her of her individuality or sense of self.

Initially, the brother's energy is instrumental in removing the sister from this destructive force. His presence in her life alters as the tale progresses, but her connection to him remains a vital force throughout her development.

The close relationship of bonding and its encounter with negative parental forces is a common motif or theme in many brother-sister tales: In the beloved Grimms' tale, "Hansel and Gretel,"[3] in which the primary focus is the brother-sister bond, the brother and sister are cast out of their parental home by their mother, who convinces their father that they can't afford to feed the children. In the course of their struggles, Hansel and Gretel each alternately take the role of leader, staying together and supporting each other through their exile. Early in the tale, Hansel, like the brother in "Brother and Sister," also takes his sister by the hand, comforts her, and attempts to save them both. Later, it is Gretel who comes up with a clever plan to save them from the witch.

Similar themes also arise in the Filipino tale "Juan and Maria"[4] (a tale much like "Hansel and Gretel"). The brother Juan finds fruit and gives it to his hungry sister Maria after they have been sent away by their parents. The brother and sister are linked, and what happens to one directly affects the other.

In all these tales, the brother is the initiator at first, but does not remain in that role through the whole tale. These tales depict a young brother-sister pair setting out on their own, in an act of faith (mingled with desperation) that is not common to children of such tender years. This motif emphasizes a powerful aspect of the special bond between the siblings, namely, that *the strong brother-sister relationship gives the two faith in their own lives.* This faith stands out in contrast to the life-denying energy of the negative mother, an energy that says "life is over"

---

[3] Brothers Grimm, No. 15, pp. 86-94.
[4] Dean S. Fansler, ed., "Juan and Maria," in *Filipino Popular Tales* (Hatboro, PA: Folklore Associates, 1965 [1921]), pp. 295-301.

whenever it makes contact with the pair. Because of the bond, a brother's sister has an inner sense of the ongoing process of life, even against strong odds. Early in the tale, the sister in "Brother and Sister" sees even the rain as *validating* her own experience when she says, "heaven and our hearts are weeping together." She believes in herself, and she also believes in a "oneness" with the world.

Her faith arises from the energy of the Self, and it carries a sense of authority. Together, brother and sister function without parental or outside authority figures. They are companion-authorities for each other. For a brother's sister, authority may be projected on her actual brother at times. However, the mutuality of this does not allow a one-sidedness for long. In most brother-sister relationships, the sister eventually will wield her own authority as well. Whatever trials the sister must go through, if she can reach inside herself deeply enough, she will be able to re-connect with the faith in her life that this strong relationship with her brother has given her. At a deep level, this faith is also a connection to her "questing spirit."[5]

2. THE FAMILY ARCHETYPES IN CONFLICT

In "Brother and Sister," the siblings have no positive parental figure. The stepmother wishes to destroy them both. She is a powerful destructive force that shows up most prominently at the beginning and at the end of the tale, though her influence is felt throughout.

This motif of parental jealousy or rejection, seen in the stepmother in "Brother and Sister," shows up over and over in brother-sister fairy tales. It is a symbolic statement about the struggle between the brother-sister pair and other archetypal energies. In fact, most brother-sister fairy tales contain either hostile, absent, or ineffectual parents. In some fairy tales, a weak father is married to a non-nurturing woman, who may be a witch, a murderess, or often, as in "Brother and Sister," a wicked stepmother who mistreats the siblings. In others, it is the father who rejects, exiles, or wishes to kill the brother and sister. In still other variations, the parents play

---

[5] This concept will receive much attention later in the book. Basically, the questing spirit is an expression of an inner creative harmony stemming from the brother-sister archetype, and it is reminiscent of the energy of the *coniunctio* sought by the alchemists. In analytic work, a dawning awareness of one's questing spirit may mark the beginning of a woman's *inner* transformation of her brother-sister energy.

no significant part in the story at all, as if they did not exist or were
of no particular consequence.

It is plausible to interpret parental negativity or absence as a
response to the brother-sister archetype itself. I am suggesting that
the mother and father imagos have an inherent hostility and envy
toward the brother-sister pair. This is not a far-fetched suggestion.
Parents are often jealous of their offspring and their accomplishments
or relationships. The parent sees his or her life slipping away, while
the new generation carries all the possibility for the future. On a strictly
inner level, we can see how our own established views fight against a
new way of thinking, feeling, or seeing the world because it threatens
our comfortable position of certainty about the world around us. The
brother-sister pair represents this new way.

Hostility and envy rise up in the parental realm both in fairy
tales in which the brother-sister relationship is strong early in the
story, as in "Brother and Sister," and in others where barely a hint
of brother-sister relationship exists initially. What is this hostility that
the parents feel towards their own offspring? Where and why does
it originate?

The brother-sister tales often provide either no explanation or
unsatisfying ones as to why the parents reject one or both of the
siblings: the father wanted to give all of his riches to his daughter so
he rejected her brothers, the stepmother hurt the children because
she was jealous of them, the parents had to kick the children out of
the house because there wasn't enough food for everyone. These
reasons—even when viewed archetypally as overvaluing the feminine
principle, envy in the negative mother-complex, a dearth of psychic
energy—do not sufficiently explain why the often-violent hostility is
directed at the brother-sister unit. It is as though the fairy tales are
dealing with what von Franz calls a "just-so" situation. The image of
brother-sister union is simply unacceptable to the mother and/or father
imagos; it is just so.

I have an inkling that the "just-so" quality of the situation can be
explained a little further. According to Kerényi, the brother-sister pair
is the originating principle in psychic consciousness (for example, Zeus
and Hera, the brother-sister pair who ruled over the other gods and
goddesses in the Greek pantheon); they are the primordial *father and
mother*, heaven and earth, "the mythological origin and beginning of

everything."[6] They exist in harmony and equality in the archetypal realm not fully available to human consciousness. They bring psychic energy together, propel us into a rebirth experience. So where is the tendency in us, as in the parental figures in the fairy tales, to so easily become estranged from our brother-sister origins? How does the split-off force of those parents find expression in our everyday lives and in our culture?

In our civilization, harmony and equality are not valued as highly as mastery and supremacy. Harmony and equality are even viewed by many as signs of weakness. Our civilization compartmentalizes and categorizes the elements in its environment, keeping those elements in a hierarchical relationship rather than unified. This is a useful tool for advancement, but we humans are so prone to identify with our work, that we *become* the compartments, estranged from their origins. We may identify with "father" or "mother"—they have power, they are big, strong compartments. But brother and sister are seen as either powerless or suspect—we no longer experience that harmonious energy as an "originating principle."

In the fairy tales, mothers and fathers are hostile toward these siblings. They are split off from their own brother-sister origins and jealous of the potential unity they see in the pair. We are all prone to experience the limited vision of these "parents." We cast a suspicious eye on our own desire for companionship and harmony, anticipating that it will mean "giving in" or losing ground.

If, in fact, we accept the Greek belief that a fundamental archetypal pattern underlying human consciousness is brother-sister union, then "mothers" and "fathers" were originally "sisters" and "brothers." The jealousy and hostility that parents in the fairy tales express toward their children may be seen as symptoms rising out of the loss of this original union, or the pain of seeing oneself replaced by a new generation of brothers and sisters. The pain is projected onto the newly forming brother-sister union in the form of jealousy and hatred.

My explanation is very different from the views—one could even say "non-views"—traditionally found in analytic and psychoanalytic theory, which tend to see brother and sister, more often than not,

---

[6] Carl Kerényi, *Zeus and Hera: Archetypal Image of Father, Husband and Wife* (Princeton, NJ: Princeton University Press, 1975), p. 96. See my discussion of this work in the Selected Annotated Bibliography, p. 199.

functioning as parental substitutes for each other.[7] Instead, as I see it, the mother and father are fragments of a broken or imperfect brother-sister union. In their struggle against their brother-sister offspring, "mother" and "father" are experiencing their own loss of that union as well as a fear of being replaced by the new pair.

In "Brother and Sister," the struggle takes shape as a negative mother seeking to destroy the pair. Her opposition increases their need for a strong bond—they have only each other—*and* it puts a curse of enchantment on that bond. This is the dual purpose of the enchantment, always experienced as a paradox.[8]

The curse to the tale's heroine is her separation from her own feminine heritage, which is passed on from mother to daughter. The black-or-white struggle orchestrated by the negative mother forces the young girl to choose between mother and brother, putting her in a delicate position. In the tale, "brother" engenders a sense of togetherness, and "mother" engenders a sense of hostility. For safety, the sister must forgo her feminine heritage.

In that moment when the female ego chooses "brother," her future is determined. She is giving the mother a rain check, and her choice is the "right" one. Just as right, however, is the fact that someday she must go back to the mother and take up her feminine struggle. Thus, the sister in the tale experiences the curse of the negative mother twice, once when she attempts to escape from the mother's dominion and again when she later becomes a mother herself.

Sister's unique nature

A young (in spirit) brother's sister is often pompous and condescending toward many of the typically "female ways." She avoids the pursuits of other women, usually feeling happiest in the company of men. She takes a not-so-secret pleasure in the jealousy of women towards her easy way of relating to men, and she scoffs at the pettiness of these women. This pompousness comes from her questing spirit (see footnote, p. 41), undeveloped as it is at this point. She may dream that she is a boy, and her energy seems that of a young androgynous being.

---

[7] See the Selected Annotated Bibliography for some notable recent exceptions to this "tendency." (Bank and Kahn, Mitchell, Cicirelli, Sanders).

[8] See p. 29.

But this energy *is* young, split off from nurture, and she carries an inner burden far older. She carries a deep and private pain, often not even known to herself, a pain associated with the inner mother who was left behind. Her pompousness is often merely a mask for that pain. She has yet to face the mother's return.

Brother appears to be a force that goes out into the world, often beckoning to sister or taking her along. What about sister's nature? Specific information about her comes as the children walk in the rain. Away from the mother's realm, sister's individual traits begin to emerge. She says, "Heaven and our hearts are weeping together." This statement reveals a keen ability to connect the natural and spiritual worlds, symbolized by rain and heaven, an ability the girl possesses throughout the tale.

The sister in this tale always first expresses a powerful connection to the natural world (rain, brooks, the forest). She has a well-developed feminine quality of receptivity. Erich Neumann[9] called this particular aspect of the feminine the "elementary character." His theory would suggest that when the sister makes a connection between natural and spiritual worlds, the "transformative character" of the feminine is trying to emerge. At this early stage, the sister in the tale can safely express a passive or receptive (elementary) aspect of her feminine nature. The transformative aspect is less developed and appears mainly as a foreshadowing of what she is to become. For the most part, the transformative feminine energy is caught in the negative mother-complex and controlled by the witchy mother. The strength of a brother's sister in the bonding stage comes predominantly from the brother-sister relationship itself, not from her feminine grounding.

3. THE STRUGGLE WITH ENCHANTMENT

On the second morning in the tale, the "new life" journey on which the brother and sister have just embarked is threatened by their stepmother, from whom they cannot separate completely. We now learn that she is a sorceress of the dark arts and intends to thwart their escape through her magical powers. This is the negative mother

---

[9] Erich Neumann, *The Great Mother* (Princeton, NJ: Princeton University Press, 1955), pp. 24-38.

complex, sneaking onto the scene and wreaking havoc as the young pair try to get away from her to find peace and harmony. Anyone who has struggled with a negative mother complex knows this experience. The very moment when it seems that some distance from the complex has been realized, the inner voice of the negative mother enters into consciousness and says, "You don't have what it takes," or something else that impedes the conscious feeling of success. A young brother's sister knows and fears this voice.

This next movement in the tale, which takes place during the brook scenes, foreshadows the separation and wound that is to come later in the brother-sister relationship. It is a complicated and important part of the story with three energies vying with each other—those of the brother, sister, and the negative mother.

Tension between brother and sister mounts during these scenes. They want different things. Brother is thirsty and wants to drink from one of the brooks, and Sister, hearing the mother's subversive message in the brooks, tries to talk him out of it. Water, the very source of life, has been contaminated by the witch, and sister and brother appear to be caught in the tension of a no-win situation. Sister's primary response to the tension at this point is fear because she knows the negative mother's tricks and foresees what might happen. She is fearful of these tricks, as though they will control her, because she cannot yet see the possibility of transformation that lies within them. Her weakness serves the dark mother, who also doesn't see or desire the possibility of transformation, but only wishes for her own supremacy. Brother's response to the tension is a mixture of desire and frustration. He lacks his sister's keen awareness of the dangers posed by the negative mother, just as she lacks his drive. At this stage in the relationship, brother and sister are immature and lacking in depth. They are children "playing at" being on their own. This is typical of the bonding stage, which is essentially an immature time, though one of great power and one in which a tendency exists for the siblings to idealize their relationship. In the brook scenes, this relationship is tested for the first time, and the tests encountered serve to either break the will or lead to the development of a depth of character. The sister must hold the tension between her idealizing tendency and the negative mother's message—"you will be destroyed"—in order to gain the depth of character to which these tests can lead her. This is an archetypal experience of tension between staying in "the garden" of innocence and moving into the world of experience, or growing up. For the brother and sister, the garden is their bond, and the sister is struggling with her own fear, symbolized by the witch stepmother, that growing up will destroy this important connection. For the "witch," that connection *has* been lost. In the depth of character that eventually develops out of this experience, the sister's questing spirit will begin to take shape.

Unlike Sister, Brother is unaware of the witch's negative influence in the forest. As on the previous day, when the pair left home, he simply takes Sister by the hand and leads her, this time to water. His movement toward water is in keeping with his active nature. Water is a primary source of life and a symbol of the unconscious. It can be experienced as either positive or negative. Jung has said that "water is that which kills and vivifies."[10] In approaching the brooks with his sister, the brother makes a move toward life, an indication of the need for more energy, or life, in their relationship.

Viewed as the masculine energy in the psyche of a female, the "brother," by leading his sister to the brooks, is symbolically directing her toward a fast-moving, bubbly, creative way of being. Neumann says that brooks are "bisexual and male and worshiped as fructifiers and movers."[11] The brother is doing what a woman's masculine energy can do so well—moving her on in a creative direction. He is even impatient for this movement to occur quickly. However, the negative mother's influence has contaminated this process and the brother, being unaware of her dark power, is more susceptible to it than his sister is. Again, looking at him as an inner experience, he is the side of the woman or young girl that would move her forward, but perhaps with not enough attention to her own safety.

The sister becomes keenly aware of the witch's negative influence over the brooks because she has a gift, an almost seer-like connection to the natural world. Also, being female, she is innately more suspicious of the negative mother than her brother. We see this kind of dynamic occurring in everyday life quite often. The man perhaps doesn't see the underlying deceitfulness of another woman, while the woman sees right through it. This difference between brother and sister is experienced as emotional tension and the fear of separation, although they stay together physically. The sister's attention is drawn to the

[10] *CW* 16 § 454.
[11] Neumann, p. 48.

messages from the negative mother, and she is not in tune with the brother's desire for water, nor does she appear to desire it herself. Psychologically, for a young brother's sister, this desire for "water," for life energy, may be projected onto the actual brother entirely or remain hidden in her unconscious animus urges. Although she will need to become conscious of her own need for the water of life later in her psychological development, this is not her task at this point. Now, the sister's role is that of mediator between brother's impulsiveness and the dangers arising from the negative mother that are lurking behind the scenes.

The negative mother has crept into the forest and enchanted all the brooks. As a mother, even a negative one, she has an inherent connection to the life source and to nature. (Later in the tale, she will again use water—in the sister's bath—for ill purposes). She can give life and she can destroy it. She *knows* how to contaminate psychic energy, and she wishes to contaminate the psychic energy of the brother-sister pair before they usurp her seat of power in the psyche. She is an archetypal force split off from the sister's consciousness, yet wanting to control her. She now seeks this control through the enchantment of the brother.

The brother *will* be enchanted. It cannot be avoided. This has been arranged through the old mother, the dark transformative aspect of the archetypal feminine. Although the sister tries to prevent it, there is a psychological need that is greater than her resistance, and it is also ultimately greater than the dark mother's evil motives: the psyche's need for growth and transformation. Enchantment serves that need, even though that is not the witch's intention. However, at this point in the story, the progressive aspects of the enchantment are not yet known; instead it would seem that in seeking to be vivified, the brother has inadvertently gone right back into the mother's snare. This type of event occurs often in fairy tales, as in life. The character appears to be losing ground, even regressing, but the temporary setback eventually brings just what the situation needs in order to move forward.

A weakness of the brother-sister relationship in the bonding stage is that while it is filled with possibility, little has been consciously actualized. The female ego must be strong to work through this stage, but that ego is not very well developed at this point. And, though the brother and sister are bonded to each other, the brother's sister has not yet harnessed or canalized[12] the energy of that bond. *The energy of the Self, imaged in a brother-sister pair seeking its own actualization, must finally help her in this struggle.*

We as adults sometimes feel that youngsters must have a guardian angel that watches over and protects them through the dangers and risks of growing up. Or maybe it's a miracle. The miracle, in the case of Sister and Brother, is likely the "guardian" that comes from the deep experience of Self that the image of the brother-sister relationship has evoked. It is strong, but the young person's conscious understanding of it is not.

The witch mother knows to strike where the early brother-sister bond is weak. As a power-driven complex, her intention is to "rule" the psyche. However, she is threatened by the relationship between the brother and sister, by the bond itself, and this is *her* weakness. *In relation to the unity implicit in their image,* she is merely a fragment of some ancient brother-sister union, the original mother and father. Her desire to enchant is accomplished. But this enchantment does not destroy. She has actually sown the seeds of transformation.

The incest threat from the Great Mother

The level of psychic consciousness or of ego development in the bonding stage is distinctly pre-adolescent, no matter what the chronological age of the brother or sister. The sister is sexually immature and cannot connect to sexuality without the fear of annihilation. This is a concrete danger for the nascent female, as well as a symbolic danger for developing feminine potential. Being "deflowered" too early is a severe wound to the feminine principle. This reality is symbolically emphasized in the fairy tale by the tiger and wolf which the brother would turn into if he drank from the first two brooks: the sexuality that is so much a part of chthonic energy (the siblings *are* in the wild) can only be experienced negatively at this time either as fragmentation—being torn apart by the wild tiger— or merging—being devoured by the wolf.

These two animals that the stepmother tries (unsuccessfully) to transform Brother into offer some insights into her motives and the

---

[12] "Canalize" means to channel or direct.

sexual issues that can be transmitted from parent to child at this stage of the brother-sister relationship. The tiger and the wolf are similar in that they are both aggressive and powerful carnivorous beasts, and their aggression is often linked in the human mind to wild sexual passions. Note how an extremely sexy woman may be called a "tigress," or how a man seeking sexual contact may be called a "prowling wolf." Symbolically and mythologically, both animals are also frequently connected to overpowering feminine energy,[13] and it is the overpowering feminine energy of the negative mother that most frightens the sister.

What does the imagery associated with the tiger and wolf suggest? I see premature sexual exposure, often in the form of incest, as carrying two possible dangers to the psyche; one is fragmentation and the other is its opposite, regression to a uroboric-like state, a symbiotic merging of psychic energies. The difference, as seen by Sister in the tale, between the tiger and the wolf is that the tiger will "tear her to pieces" and the wolf will "devour her." These are the psychological states that result from incest, whether it is predominantly psychological, spiritual, or physical in nature. When the negative mother poses this threat by trying to turn the brother into a wolf or tiger, she is attempting to dominate the psychic life of the individual. The sister would truly become her "daughter" were either of these transformations to take place.

The threat of the tiger and wolf alerts us that there is a risk of overpowering sexual expression coming from the outside which could impose itself on the brother-sister bond at this stage. The particular risk comes from the insinuation of the negative mother energy through the unconscious. In fact, the incest threat which comes from the mother realm is quite different from that which arises from the brother-sister bond itself.[14] It is the danger of enchantment, which results in a clouding of consciousness. Because the sister becomes keenly aware of these threats, she helps her brother navigate through the first two

---

[13] "Little Red Riding Hood," in which a young girl's grandmother is eaten by a wolf, who then eats the girl while disguised as the grandmother, is the classic tale of "the deadly, devouring mother" (*CW* 17 § 219n). The tiger is considered one of the "transformations of the Great Goddess" (de Vries, p. 467), which means that goddesses are known to transform into this animal in multiple cultures.

[14] The incestuous energy arising from the brother-sister bond will be discussed at length in Chapter 14.

dangers posed by the wolf and tiger. She sees these dangers as life-threatening; and, indeed, incest is a threat to progression in the life of the psyche. The whole psychic life of the individual "goes dead" in a regressed state, if incest takes over.

Actual incest, in fact, is often experienced as a kind of psychological death, in which movement outward—into the embrace of the "otherness" of the world—is stopped. For example, in the Russian fairy tale, "Prince Danila Govorila,"[15] the risk of incest that is imposed on the brother and sister by a mother figure is at the heart of the tale. A witch gives the old mother of the siblings a ring, saying that the brother will prosper if he marries the girl whom the ring fits. The ring fits only his sister, and so he asks her to marry him. The sister's response to his proposal is compatible with the sister's instinctive response in "Brother and Sister." She sees incest as a threat to her being and seeks help to escape the marriage bed. In this Russian tale, resolution comes when the sister goes on a journey into the underworld and brings back to her brother another woman, her double in many respects, who becomes his bride.

When a woman experiences masculine energy in the form of invasion, a balanced union of masculine and feminine energies within her psyche is severely thwarted. Jung refers to this condition in his own discussion of "Prince Danila Govorila" when he says that for the brother, marriage to the sister is "an evil fate that cannot easily be avoided."[16] I would say that the brother unconsciously longed for the bond of the brother-sister union, and in the case of "Prince Danila Govorila," the witchy feminine (again the dark mother) charmed him into thinking that the actualization of this bond would give him power. Prosperity and power are what she promises him if he weds the woman whom the ring fits.

It seems to be inherent in the human condition—call it our fate—that we cannot stay in the state of unconscious union, be it brother-sister union or some other *participation mystique*. We must become conscious of this state, or at some point it will cease to be beneficial. The brother and sister of "Prince Danila Govorila" have reached that point psychologically. Marriage is presented as "literal"

---

[15] Aleksandr Afanas'ev, coll., "Prince Danila Govorila," in *Russian Fairy Tales* (New York: Pantheon Books, 1973 [1945]), pp. 351-356.

[16] *CW* 16 § 431.

marriage because they are developmentally ready for it. The *choice* of marriage partner is the focus. In "Brother and Sister," the development of the two energies is such that they are not ready for union at a "higher level"—i.e., sacred marriage—until later in the tale. The siblings need to stay a while longer in the state of brother-sister bonding. It is the dark force outside them that attempts to force the "wild beasts" on them. Later, when she is ready, marriage will come to the sister in a quite different form.

It is the witch's intention, in both "Brother and Sister" and "Prince Danila Govorila," that Sister and Brother should fall victim to the fate of incestuous union, and therefore not be able to maintain a positive connection. If brother "gives in" to the fate, it will severely damage the sister's ego and animus development. Also, the premature destruction of the brother-sister bond would constitute a loss of soul, or a loss of soulful connection within the psyche of the girl. There is a strong bond personified by the brother-sister pair, and forced union would damage that bond. The union must come from within the relationship itself and must develop in its own time. They, the pair, must hold steady with the tension in their relationship (that of wanting two seemingly opposite things) so that psychological development, and not psychological incest, may occur.

In his study of the transference phenomenon, Jung makes a statement about brother-sister incest (in the context of discussing images of alchemical symbolism) that symbolically carries this incest theme to an even deeper psychological level. I believe we too must go to that deeper level in our exploration of the theme:

> As regards the psychology of this [brother-sister] pair, we must stress above all else that it depicts a human encounter where love plays the decisive part. ... Although the union of close blood-relatives is everywhere taboo, it is yet the prerogative of Kings (witness the incestuous marriages of the Pharaohs, etc.). Incest symbolizes union with one's own being, it means individuation or becoming a self, and, *because this is so vitally important, it exerts an unholy fascination*—not, perhaps, as a crude reality, but certainly as a psychic process controlled by the unconscious, a fact well known by anybody who is familiar with psychopathology.[17]

---

[17] *CW* 16 § 419.

The italics here are mine. These words carry profound implications for relations between the individual psyche and the collective[18] of which he/she is a part, as well as for relations between brother and sister (inner and outer). When dealing with actual cases of physical incest, it is nearly impossible to get to the psychological level that Jung alludes to in this quote. The concretization of the incest thwarts psychological transformation. It is only long after the wounds of invasion and false merger (that is, a merger forced on the developing psyche) are healed that we can go to where Jung is leading us in this passage. Jung's focus here is on the psychological transformation that is required of us by the incest taboo. Jung and Layard both actually see the incest taboo as a mandate from the unconscious psyche which forces us to develop a psychological relationship to the "other" as an inner figure.[19]

In seeking consciousness, the psyche, as the fairy tales indicate, abhors (and is secretly drawn to) the *idea* of incest, because if acted upon, incest practically cuts off the chances for the psyche to come into its own fullness. The threat of a concrete incestuous relationship is powerful in many siblings' lives and will be addressed in more depth in later chapters. Symbolically, incest projects out into the world of "crude reality" the secret, which the psyche must keep protected and sheltered if it is to thrive. That secret is "union with one's own being," the Self-experience often symbolized by the brother-sister pair. The Self threatens to take the individual into a private world; while the outside world exerts an equal and opposite pull. This creates tension within the psyche. The collective world can never fully condone the inward-energy that union with the Self demands. Anyone who has gone off on an individual quest that was different from what others expected of him or her knows the pain of this tension.

If the mother's early incest threats (seen in her attempts to transform the brother in "Brother and Sister" into a tiger or wolf) had been realized, the "bonding" stage would have been severely damaged. In this particular tale, if one of the *purposes* of the enchantment (the reinforcing of the bond) is to be served, the brother must not become a tiger or wolf. As either of these animals, he would be in the dark Great Mother's power, and might carry out her wishes to destroy the

---

[18] Collective consciousness, or "the collective," refers to the outer psychological reality—the culture, social or religious group—in which the individual lives.
[19] See Selected Annotated Bibliography, pp. 198-200.

young developing feminine energy. Sexual aggression, brought on through "possession" by the negative mother archetype, would have wiped out any hope of transformation.

Once negative mother energy has assumed the form of a powerful witch, she wishes to destroy anyone who will not preserve and further her own power. She no longer has the capacity to experience the union of opposites; all she knows is the destructive power of the beasts. In her narrow vision, she is the dark shadow side of the sister's own tendency toward one-sidedness. The sister clearly is potential "victim" in this tale, but as is often true of victims, her own narrow focus sometimes limits her ability to perceive her options. For example, she has a "nothing-but" attitude to the tiger, wolf, and roebuck. That is, she sees only the negative potential (as her stepmother also does) in these transformations. The sister passively foresees her own doom, and the stepmother actively plans it. Eventually, sister will need to deal with this shadow side of her own feminine nature. But now is not the time.

In this fairy tale, brother and sister are children, but the psychic energies that they, the mother, and the beasts represent are alive and vying with one another in individuals of all ages. Witness the dream brought to me recently by a successful and intelligent woman in her mid-forties:

I was 12 years old, and I was alone in our house at night. My mother had gone to a school meeting with my older brother. I loved our little white brick house. It was like a cottage. I was anxious and frightened to be alone. I felt something awful was going to happen. I wondered why I felt so scared in this house that I loved so much. I checked all of the doors to make sure they were locked. When my mother and brother came home, they found obscene notes scattered around the house and spray-painted on the sidewalks. The notes were about me. I was very frightened. My brother and I checked all of the doors and windows to make sure they were all locked. I knew that whoever had written the notes was lurking in the dark near our house. My brother and I decided to go to bed, and went through a kind of enclosed breezeway to get to the part of the house where the bedrooms were. The large, dark, wooden, sliding doors on one side of the breezeway were unlocked. This made me uncomfortable, because I knew someone could get in this way. They locked from the outside and, if we locked them, my brother would be locked outside and I would have to go to the front door and let him in. Besides, our grandmother was at a neighbor's house telling them about the notes and we didn't know if she had a key, so we left the doors unlocked. The plan was for me to sleep in my mother's room that night with her. My brother said for me to go up to her room and he would check all of the doors and windows in that part of the house. I went to my mother's room. It was a long room with two twin beds. I called for my mother and she didn't answer. Then I heard the shower running and figured she was in there. I went into the bathroom and called "mother" several times. Suddenly a male figure pulled back the shower curtains. He lunged at me with a knife in one hand and whispered "python." I'm not sure if he had a python around one hand or had a python head for his head. I ran in terror back into the bedroom and saw my brother's face at the window. He had locked himself out of the house and couldn't get back in.

This woman has no actual brother, and her positive mother-complex had supported her well through the first half of her life. The "house that I loved so much" symbolizes this positive complex which has now become ominous and filled with portent. Recently she had been depressed and confused about the "rightness" of some of her major decisions. This dream came to her during this time. Archetypally, the dream addresses aspects of the brother-sister bond, the negative or deceptive mother (the shadow side of her positive mother-complex), and invasion from the water (shower) by a beast who is connected to the mother (it appears in her bathroom). It is striking that these are the same themes that appear in the brook scenes of "Brother and Sister."

However, in this woman's dream, an actual separation from the brother occurs, and the feminine ego is in a dangerous spot. Actual separation from the brother is a very real possibility in the course of a sister's development, and, although it did not occur in "Brother and Sister," it does happen in the English fairy tale "The Laidly Worm of Spindleston Heugh" (discussed in Chapter 8). In that tale, the brother goes off to seek his fortune without his sister, and their evil stepmother turns his sister into a "laidly worm," or dragon. She is restored to her human form only when her valiant brother returns and is willing to kiss the laidly worm instead of following his first instinct to slay it. Here we see again that the experience of brother-sister union or reunion can break through the enchantment imposed by the negative mother. The enchantment itself can be seen as having served the purpose of the tale in that it reunited the brother and sister.

In my client's dream, the energies that arise are moving her toward transformation, and this feels threatening and dangerous to her. This woman has a powerful negative animus (here he has darkened the mother-experience), and the brother-figure for her was a new and welcomed positive masculine image. But, as the brother's face at the window graphically attests, separation from this new energy could occur in the twinkling of an eye, and the negative forces (depression and indecision) are waiting to envelop her. She must consciously do the work of the brother's sister, struggling with the darkness and reuniting with her companion.

Likewise, in "Brother and Sister," the sister feels threatened by the enchantment. This is her negative mother-complex speaking, the inner voice that limits her experience. The sister has exhibited a feminine wisdom, but when speaking from within the narrow vision of her complex, she would have the brother never taste life, and consequently never lead her into it.

At the third brook, brother and sister finally are given over to the fate of their enchantment. They have struggled with each other in a "tension of the opposites," and at the end of this struggle, the brother has been transformed, not into a tiger or wolf, but into a roebuck.

4. THE ROEBUCK-BROTHER

The "choice" the brother makes to become a roebuck when he drinks from the third brook gives him what "they" (the inner brother-sister pair) need. This transformation is necessary and represents a new psychological possibility. It is time for the brother-sister pair to learn about the nature of the roebuck and for the sister to learn about her roebuck-brother as an inner figure in her psyche. (It may be easier, in fact, for us to see the brother-roebuck as an aspect of the developing young woman, rather than as a separate person.)

The brother-roebuck is a wild creature of the forest—cunning, sure-footed, and elusive. Being young, he lacks the masculine strength associated with the mature roebuck, but this strength exists as a potential within him, and therefore within the psyche. In the course of the story, the roebuck develops some of that potential, although we never see him develop into a full male deer. The emphasis of the story is on the sister's development.

As an expression of the brother-animus in a young brother's sister, the young roebuck, who is "bashful" and knows how to stay hidden from human eyes, initially represents the sister's own skittishness with regard to the outside world. That outside world is personified by the male hunters who appear later in the story. However, after the pair have lived in the protected forest for a long time, this skittish aspect of the brother-roebuck is no longer a focus. Instead, a new instinct emerges as the brother-roebuck begins to draw his sister into involvement with the outside world. Hidden within the young roebuck's being is the transformative energy of the antlers,[20] and when that manifests, he leads his sister to her next transformation.

Jung describes a roebuck in the story of Hiawatha:

> Further, the roebuck was no ordinary animal, but a magic one with an unconscious (i.e., symbolical) significance. Hiawatha made himself gloves and moccasins from its hide: the gloves gave such power to his arms that he could crumble rocks to dust, and the moccasins had the virtue of seven-leagued boots. By clothing himself in the hide he became a sort of giant. Therefore the roebuck killed at the ford was a "doctor animal," a magician who had changed his shape, or a daemonic being—a symbol, that is to say, which points to the "animal" and other such powers of the unconscious.[21]

The roebuck-brother in "Brother and Sister," like the roebuck in the Hiawatha story, is a magical beast of the unconscious. He differs from the roebuck in Hiawatha in that his roebuck form has been imposed upon him from the outside by the stepmother, whereas in Hiawatha a magician has transformed himself into a roebuck. The actions the roebuck takes and why he takes them, which cannot be understood through reason, eventually have a magical or transformative significance for the sister; this is inevitable.

Shortly after the brother is turned into a roebuck, the sister gives him her golden garter and weaves a leash for him: they are once more

---

[20] Antlers are related to transformation in several respects: Unlike horns, they change and re-grow each year; they only develop in the animal's adulthood and are an indication of his age; and, in ancient times they were seen as "antennae" to the otherworld.
[21] *CW* 5 § 503.

in a brother-sister union. In these acts she now embodies the potential of an Artemis figure.[22] Artemis is a nature Goddess and the twin sister of Apollo. She is an expression of harmony in the brother-sister union. She also has a strong link to the deer of the forest, and she even places a gold bridle, like the sister's golden garter, on deer in the forest. In "Brother and Sister," the enchantment has given sister (as well as brother) a chance to connect to new inner potential and to grow with it. For the time being, it serves also to strengthen their bond.

What about the negative mother and her relationship to the enchantment? Later in the story we learn that once she bewitched the brooks, she thought her work was done. In a sense, she was right—in that she had transformed the brother into a form that would lead to the sister's psychological development. However, this was clearly not the mother's intention. And, ironically, her violent power is also temporarily modified once brother becomes a roebuck. He has become not only an animal with magical and transformative significance, but one who can also continue to be in relationship with the sister. This, of course, was not the negative mother's intention either.

At this point, the relationship's successful continuation depends on the sister's response to the roebuck. The sister's early Artemis-like behavior toward the roebuck indicates that the enchantment awakened *within her* the image of the divine brother-sister union, since Artemis is herself part of a harmonious brother-sister union. The internalization of this image of union is an essential step in the sister's development because it allows her to move from a concrete relationship to a symbolic one with the brother. Adult sisters can often look back and recognize early experiences of this psychological moment: brother is not available as he once was, and now the girl must be her own brother. Only in hindsight do we understand that this is what happened.

The enchantment also imposes severe limits on the brother-sister relationship and bond. Staying together now will require more conscious effort on the part of both sister and brother. Because of his

---

[22] The sister's Artemisian potential was suggested early in the tale by her relationship to the natural world (rain) and understanding of the voices in nature (the brooks). I was struck, when reading material on Artemis, to find this passage in an essay by Tom Moore: "Artemis goes out and finds deer whose horns 'shine gold,' puts golden bridles on them and harnesses them to her vehicle"—Tom Moore, "Artemis and the Puer," *Puer Papers* (Irving, TX: Spring Publications, 1979), p. 178. This is a bold parallel to the actions of the young sister when brother becomes a roebuck.

new roebuck nature, the brother will want to bound away. Thus, the golden garter and leash are not only symbolic of sister's budding Artemis nature, but also of her conscious efforts to maintain what might be a fragile connection with her roebuck-brother.

Now she may learn to recognize, or become conscious of, the relationship in which she had previously been only unconsciously involved. In the past, the brother led and she followed. However, at this point in the story's development, the sister takes on the role of protector and even, to some extent, that of initiator. Previously, she was worried that *he* would leave her; now she promises that *she* will never leave him. She leads him with the leash she has made.

We see this process, in which the sister starts to take actions that her brother had traditionally taken, in many of the brother-sister fairy tales. Brother may be the authority or the leader, then at another time sister assumes these roles. For example, in "Hansel and Gretel" (another tale about the brother-sister bond, which was mentioned earlier), brother is the planner and comforter until they reach the witch's hut. Then, sister becomes an initiator and eventually out-tricks the witch. Authority switches from one to the other.

At this point in "Brother and Sister," the tale enters one of its two phases of peaceful, harmonious existence. The sister and brother live in a little cottage in the woods, and they are happy "for some time." The brother's roe-form is the only blight to their happiness. A balance between conscious and unconscious has been reached, albeit a precarious one. The roe is tame and acts as a support for his sister— his back is her pillow.

Developmentally, this period parallels the latter part of pre-adolescence. Brother and sister are still in a child-like bonded state with simple needs. As they grow, the pressure to move beyond their cottage in the woods will mount, but for now there is peace. In the course of a woman or a man's life, even after they have left this protected psychological space, they may still return to it from time to time. This space is not chronologically bound to a pre-adolescent period, but is a psychological configuration in the life of an individual. It provides a safe place where transformation can occur, free from the demands of the outer world. It is a place and time of almost uroboric harmony. Though the brother's roe-form is a haunting reminder of the negative mother, it also provides needed energy and instruction for the pair, so that even the witch can be forgotten for a while. Here, the girl child grows into a beautiful young maiden. Men and women alike can benefit from the awareness of this peaceful space, a time when inner harmony has been achieved, and a preparation for the next psychological challenge can occur.

5. The Importance of Bonding

The stage of bonding is essential to the brother-sister relationship if it is to transform, in the woman's psyche, into an inner experience of "union with one's own being."[23] This stage provides an early experience of wholeness, of the Self. In this sense, for the girl, brother-animus and Self become psychic realities at the same time, and the female's connection to each develops side by side. The inner brother is projected onto the real or imagined brother, who is an animus figure. This process turns the archetypal image of brother-sister union into a *felt* reality for the girl/woman, and that feeling is the experience of the Self.

During the bonding stage, brother and sister struggle to separate from other powerful forces, such as the dark mother, often in order to survive. As in "Brother and Sister," they go off together to fashion a life on their own in "the wide world." Psychologically, her experience of the positive brother imago gives a woman the belief and initiative to forge her own life.

While early bonding is the expression of a "young" female's connection with the brother-animus, this bonding sometimes can become so comfortable that going out into the expansive world—the collective—presents a problem. In "Brother and Sister," the sister, safe in the little house in the woods with her roebuck brother, resists new figures entering into her life in the forest. However, this doesn't block her development because before much time has passed, her brother brings a king to her door! In some stories and lives, however, such a positive result is not achieved and the bond becomes an unhealthy block to development.

What follows bonding is wounding, and the brother's sister must go forth into the world. If the bond has been strong, it will begin to transform and remain with her as an "inner light," a beacon that keeps her in touch with her own center through life's trials, whatever they may be.

---

[23] *CW* 16 § 419.

CHAPTER SIX

Wounding

1. THE OUTSIDE WORLD COMES IN

The forest is deep and dark, and the sister and brother wander far into it before they find the house in which they live during their "peaceful time." This time is like an incubation, during which sister and roe-brother exist in an intimate relationship to each other and to nature. This time gives the individual psyche a strength that it will carry out into its worldly experiences.

The next movement in the tale is sudden and brings the outside world into the heart of the forest. A King and his huntsmen arrive in the very place where the siblings live. It is a "great hunt"; its object is no small matter. Judging from the outcome of the hunt, the King appears to have been searching for the sister and her roe. Sister has grown to be a young maiden, and the roebuck's actions in this scene are that of an animal who is now too big and active for the cottage. The brother and sister are being hunted out and beckoned to come into contact with the outer world. The time of bonding is at its end, and a new stage of development is on the horizon.

During this time, two activating forces begin to emerge in the woman's psyche: symbolically, they can be seen in the arrival of the King and the changed attitude/behavior of her roe-brother. The King is a completely new element: a change will need to occur for brother and sister to deal with him. The brother's behavior is not completely new—he has gone against his sister's wishes before when he drank from the third enchanted brook—but his actions are much more pronounced this time. He does not stay indoors even for one day, but responds immediately to the call of the hunt, although Sister tries to convince him not to. Sister's resistance is an expression of her controlling mother-complex, combined with her Artemis "purity," which rejects masculine contact.[1] These prohibiting factors merge to form a negative complex that resists expansion of the ego and resists giving up the close bond sister has with brother.

The sister's fear of the "rough huntsmen" is her "nothing-but" attitude manifesting again, this time without the support of her intuitive powers, and brother does not take it seriously. He is anxious to enter the hunt, running and engaging in sport with the hunters. There is a wisdom in the roebuck's activity, grounded in his instinctive in-tune-ness with the psyche's needs. This wisdom operates quite separately from our conscious notions about what we need. The brother does not take his sister's hand this time, as he has so often before; he instead asks to be set free.

The brother-sister tales contain differing images of the wounding stage. To understand this particular tale's image, we must examine the relationships between three figures—roe, sister, and King—at the outset of this stage:

The roebuck is very eager to engage in the hunt with the King and his huntsmen. The language used here—that the roebuck is "anxious," "cannot bear it," "had no peace," and is about to "jump out of [his] skin"—indicates that his eagerness to participate is an innately masculine—phallic and action-oriented—response. This is curious, since he is the object of the hunt and could be killed. Nevertheless, his language suggests that he can't help but be involved. The love of sport is activated in him. The sportsman knows what it is to "give them a good fight," the thrill of "going up against that team." It is this type of feeling statement that captures the energy of the roebuck's desire for the hunt. He is connected to it in a positive way, desiring what it has to offer—masculine activity and transformation.

The King is the organizer and leader of the hunt. As King, he represents the dominant conscious principle in the outer world of collective consciousness, and he brings a new and different energy to the brother-sister pair in the cottage in the woods. As the leader of

---

[1] One story tells of the severe reaction Artemis has when a young hunter, Actaeon, comes upon her bathing naked in the forest. She turns him into a stag, and he is run down and killed by his own hounds.

this hunt, he is seeking contact with them. The King is a new and compelling masculine image for the sister, and his great energy is further symbolized by the huntsmen at his side. During the hunt, the roe, the King, and the huntsmen act in such harmony with each other that they appear to have a common goal.

Symbolically, the roebuck (like the stag) and King belong together, especially if the roebuck is magical and enchanted. They are crowned masculine rulers, one above (culture, consciousness), the other below (forest, unconscious). Stag kings, or the image of king as a male deer, have been common in various European cultures (Celtic, Anglo-Saxon). The King's crown and the antlers of the deer are visually similar, and symbolically they both represent great intellectual or spiritual power. At this point in our story, the Kingdom, or psychic arena, needs this roebuck and his beautiful sister to come out of hiding as much as *they* now need to join up with the ruler of the kingdom.

The sister fears the hunters and resists contact with them. In psychological language, her conscious position, reflected in her timidity and avoidance of the King and his men, conflicts with her unconscious desire for movement and interaction. The roebuck "acts out" this desire for her, while she remains unconscious of it. The brother's role as the hunted one gives the sister a rational, conscious reason to resist the hunters: her own brother-animus stands a good chance of being hurt. She is in danger of losing "who I am" for the sake of "who I can become." The girl senses that the platonic and sheltered brother-sister relationship is in danger. She is afraid of the new way that is emerging, and she may even be ashamed of her own secret longings.

Such rational resistance often exists where psychological growth is demanded, but the unconscious urges finally cease to listen to these excuses. At the beginning of the hunt, however, the sister is not ready yet to give in. She struggles against what she perceives as an attack from the strong masculine invaders, unconscious elements in her psyche. She wants to remain undisturbed in the forest, to keep "life as it has been," but she cannot prevent the inevitable. Even her brother-animus is out of harmony with her conscious wishes. He longs for activity, involvement in the world and the hunt, the challenge of this engagement, and, ultimately, for transformation. The sister is forced to hide behind a locked door in order to avoid the King. There is activity in the animus-region, and the girl is backed into a corner.

One concrete outward manifestation of this period is adolescence. However, "adolescence," like all stages of life, is also a state of mind that is not chronologically bound and can be experienced in the psychic structure not just of young girls but in individuals at any age. At various points in a woman's life, for example, she will need to struggle for balance between her own feminine nature and vying animus energies. The struggle often has an "adolescent" feel. I have often heard an adult woman say, "I feel like a thirteen-year-old."

A young brother's sister often values the kind of connection found in the brother-sister bond and eschews the onslaught of less trustworthy involvements with masculinity. The sister's "purity" rises up in response to non-brother masculinity. In relationships with the opposite sex, she will attempt to re-enact the brother-sister model, and usually be hurt or disappointed by the "uncompanionable" nature of the males. She is a human girl with an Artemis purity about her, and she holds onto that purity in her little cottage. Brother feels safe, and if other boys or men don't act like brothers, she isolates herself, or important parts[2] of herself, from them. She may put very little of herself into these other relationships, simply going through the motions. She is unwilling to trust the non-brother masculine realm, thus putting off her own psychological development.

Either way, the sister is attempting to shut and lock the door to anyone but the roe-brother. But now, even he cannot be trusted fully as he once was. As a personification of her own masculine roe-nature, he is transforming from a shy creature into one who can bring new energy into the life of the sister. In the unconscious, a lot of energy is being stirred up, and it is only a matter of time before that locked door opens. The time has come for movement outward.

In the tale, the roe shifts the balance and precipitates this movement forward with his compulsion to join the hunt. In actual experience, a brother's sister may feel forsaken by her brother during this period. Or her own inner roe, her brother-animus, may stir up

---

[2] This "important parts" is significant. The girl may be promiscuous on the surface, but never share her innermost self with any lover. Her sexuality remains unrelated and immature or primitive. In this way, she limits her experience of the non-brother masculine, as well as limiting his experience of her.

trouble. Inner and outer reflect each other. She feels divided. She "used to know herself," but now cannot understand the stirrings and longings she is experiencing. They may feel foreign and impure to her, an experience of invasion by "rough huntsmen." The crowned King or antlered roebuck are not yet part of her experience.

A brother's sister at this stage has romanticized the bond with her brother. She holds onto her inner world of fantasy brother-sister union as a security against the invasion she fears. The thought of contact with rough masculinity is threatening, as well as secretly fascinating. The movement into new relationship needs to happen so that this split between conscious and unconscious attitudes does not intensify into a pathological condition.[3]

This tale indicates that the actual separation of a woman from her brother animus does not have to last long—just long enough to allow the new (non-brother) masculine element to enter. It may be that the girl's actual brother encourages her to meet the man who represents this new masculine energy, to get out and be involved with the world. Her inner brother—the desire for action, movement, and the thrill of the hunt—at this point is seeking that very same involvement. Consciously, she may still be trying to push down that urge, but eventually conscious and unconscious will need to get together. The tension between the two creates an opening, and that is the wound through which the new masculine energy can rise to consciousness.

As an inner aspect of a woman's psyche, the "brother" sometimes can be so connected to her and so accepting of her that she becomes quite reluctant to move out of the comfort zone he provides. An unconscious "filtering" process will take place within her, which results in repression of the masculine urges that don't fit her brother mold. These urges may come out of such experiences as exposure to excitement and risk-taking (adventure), new ideas that challenge her existing way of being (philosophy), sexual opportunity, etc. Her brother-complex will resist these new feelings and desires, labeling them unwholesome, dirty, or foolish. But, sooner or later, even the brother within will become influenced by the urges. And the chase will be on, into a new phase of her life. She is half running, half dragged, by her own internal conflicts, but she is moving into the new adventure.

---

[3] For descriptions of this kind of pathological condition, see Chapter 14 on "The Glass Coffin." See also, *The Glass Menagerie* (1945) by Tennessee Williams.

It follows that in reality every brother-sister relationship must experience a wound if the sister is to move on into her individual experience of the world. For the brother's sister, resistance to such an experience is the ego's position. She may very well believe that her whole identity is connected to that of her brother, or to that of her inner world of philosophical, pure "brother" relationships. However, if the wound in the relationship does not occur, the sister's development will be arrested in the stage of early brother-sister bonding, a form of *participation mystique.*

This kind of arrested development has devastating effects in which the psyche becomes stuck in an infantile regression of libido. Sam Shephard's play, *Fool for Love*,[4] is a dramatic enactment of these torturous effects. In the play, a brother and sister are obsessed with their incestuous union. Their futile efforts to sever their destructive bond form the tragic and repetitive action of the play.

Movement from bonding to wounding is psychologically painful, and the point when movement must begin is a fragile time. The whole wounding experience will be a growing up for the girl, a dissolution of her unconscious *participation mystique.* It is part of the first-half-of-life journey, but later that same wounding will serve as the opening back into the unconscious when the psyche's goal, individuation, has revealed itself.

In a last attempt to maintain her conscious status quo, sister gives her brother a password to get back into their cottage when he returns from the hunt: only he is given the password so that only he shall be allowed admittance to her domain. In this portion of the tale, sister becomes increasingly more debilitated, hiding in the cottage, desperately seeking a way to maintain her old pattern of existence. She is behaving like a skittish deer, just as her roebuck-brother did when he was very young, but her unconscious brother-roebuck animus has matured and is now strong and proud. The skittish deer is an imaginal representation of the tendency toward infantile regression of the libido. She wants brother "the old way." She doesn't want him to grow, she wants him to remain the timid child-roebuck.

The female caught in this struggle may be able to perform only very minimally in the outside world. All activity is internal.

---

[4] Sam Shephard, *Fool for Love* (San Francisco, CA: City Lights, 1983).

Outwardly, she is distracted, withdrawn, or lacking in energy, just "going through the motions." The inner struggle may bring on an uncharacteristic moodiness. As in the tale, there may be brief periods during which she feels or acts "like herself," when the roe comes home in the evenings. But "brother" and "sister" now are divided. The experience of tension, struggle, and resistance goes on for three days (this can feel like, or be, a lifetime); again, a three-ness is needed for the next step in psychic development.

On the first day of the hunt, the beautiful roebuck is chased but unharmed. On the second day, he is wounded a little in the foot. This slows him down, allowing a huntsman to follow him home and hear the password the brother repeats at his sister's door. The huntsman takes this information to the King.[5] On the third day of the hunt, the roe is chased, but the King himself goes to the door with the roe's password. The roe has caught the attention of the King and huntsmen, and his wound allows them to enter into the life of the brother-sister pair.

The roe catches the attention of the King because he is that lovely, swift, magical (golden collar) creature of the unconscious who draws psychic energy to himself. He leaps and bounds and begins a psychological process which no one can control. It is fitting that he should catch the King's attention because of the earlier-mentioned connection between kings and male deer (p. 63). A coming together of King and roebuck strengthens and vivifies masculine energy. It also suggests that the king is the "right" kind of king. In their unity, conscious and instinctive royalty come together; it is an "as above, so below" union that sanctifies the Kingly position. In the tale, the King has the correct attitude toward the roebuck: he engages it, is careful not to harm it, and follows where it takes him.

What of the roe's wound in the foot? Jung has said that "the foot, as the organ nearest the earth, represents in dreams relation to earthly reality and often has a generative or phallic significance."[6] The foot-wound is archetypally a masculine wound. When a man "shoots himself in the foot," the wound is to his masculinity. The roebuck-brother experiences this injury, albeit briefly, and this intensifies the need for

---

[5] This huntsman's feminine counterpart shows up in the nurse at the end of the tale. They are helpers who know where to take valuable information.

[6] *CW* 5 § 356.

the pair to join with the outside forces. The injury slows the brother down and takes away some of his sexual/creative energy, which allows the others (huntsmen and King) to discover the password, the secret brother-sister code. It is the creative potential locked in this brother-sister bond that must be revitalized and re-channeled. It is time for the brother-as-hero (bringer of new creative potential) to allow for an expansion or transformation of the sister's animus.

During the hunt, the girl's animus has been "working overtime." Symbolically, sexual energy has been high, mental activity rising, and she has had very little conscious control over it all. In fact, her consciousness has hidden away from all this energy. She is out of touch with her own changing feelings, drives, and interests because she has projected all of that on her brother. The conscious will of the sister is too defended against her unconscious side.

Because she has not allowed herself to have contact with anyone except the brother, he has necessarily carried all of this heightened energy for her. Then, he is wounded. His own phallic energy is temporarily out of commission. In this brief experience of her roe-brother's wound, the sister begins to recognize that she is isolated, with no one but him in the world. She will be "alone and forsaken" if he dies. She sees the limits of her situation. What this means psychologically for the brother's sister is that she is a step away from realizing that it is she who might need a change from the old way so that other masculine forces can become a consciously integrated part of her psyche.

The way that the King and his huntsmen plan to get into the cottage has a trickster quality to it that should not be overlooked. The King is a positive figure, but nevertheless he must trick or deceive the girl in order to gain admittance to her domain. He has only slightly wounded the roe-brother; he has but one day left to see the sister, so the sister must be tricked. These facts point to the delicacy of the transition from bonding to wounding.

There are situations in which the "right time" for psychological transition is missed. In tales such as "The Glass Coffin" (Chapter 14), the brother and sister have passed beyond the "right time," the delicate time. When the trickster invades their lives, he has turned dark and sinister, and the wounding nearly destroys them. They become "frozen" in time, she in a coffin and he as a powerful wandering stag. In this condition, they are *forced* apart. Only during that enforced separation does the sister begin to "dream up" the man who will liberate her. He is a tailor, who can sew back together her fragmented psyche after her devastating experience with the dark magician.

"Brother and Sister" presents a different situation. The fragile transition from bonding to wounding occurs at the "right" point. Even so, the sister's conscious response to the wound is to tend it, and then to try to keep the doors shut tight. This is an incestuous posture (avoiding outside energy). However, she has little conscious control over it. On the third day, the roebuck continues to act in harmony with the King by insisting on re-engaging in the hunt.

Concretely, the wounding creates a breach in the bond that allows both the brother and sister to experience new and different relationships. The King is about to appear at the cottage with the intent to marry the sister. He is the new figure that the roebuck *brings to his sister* by engaging in the hunt. The natural flow of libido in the psyche brings about their contact. Because roebuck and King are allied, the roebuck-brother becomes a transforming agent in his sister's development from maidenhood to queenly status. She is now in her final preparation to meet the King.

The King does not come to the sister until she and brother have been through three days of the hunt. In fairy tales, three is typically a number (be it of trials, questions, days) that readies the characters for the transformation. After the third day, when the King finally enters the cottage and asks the sister to marry him, she readily consents. It seems curious that a young maiden, so resistant before to the mere thought of interaction with these huntsmen, should be so willing now. However, this is often the way psychological changes happen. We resist the new attitude or new experience forcefully for a while, and then when the right time comes, the change takes place with little effort. It seems so easy! The sister has been through three days of "preparation" for the arrival of the King, each day forced to accept a little more that her roe-brother wanted what this "other world" had to offer. Finally she is ready to meet the King and the other world he represents.

The brother and sister have never been fully separated from each other during the wounding stage, and now they continue on their journey together, even as the sister embarks on her new life with the King. She makes it a condition of her marriage that her roe-brother be allowed to accompany her. In this way, she maintains her connection to him; and, again in Artemis fashion, she puts on his leash and leads him away with her and the King. The brother-sister relationship has been altered, but sister makes room for the continuation of it.

In the animus development of a brother's sister, a continual sense of connection to the inner brother is optimal. Her loyalty to that connection is a loyalty of kinship. This tale suggests that the further animus development the sister needs—that is, connection to her inner King and to her own inner boy-child—*can* take place without turning her back on the inner brother.

Typically, a sense of loyalty is strong and persistent in a brother's sister, and it is a psychological stance that any woman learns when she becomes familiar with the positive aspects of her own brother-animus. Loyalty, a factor in all the brother-sister tales, is part of the sister's "questing spirit" energy. Of course, in our lives we learn about loyalty in many ways, but the loyalty inherent in the brother-sister bond has a special quality. Brother and sister live that loyalty from a very early age because they are "in this together." Loyalty to oneself, to one's own process, no matter what the outside world may say of that process, comes from an early and profound sense of union, such as that symbolized by the brother-sister pair. Although a balance must be reached between loyalty to the bond and relationship with the outside world, if the loyalty is lost in that process, it means a loss of soul for the brother's sister. In this tale, when sister, King, and roe leave the forest, the first movement of the wounding stage in the brother-sister relationship has taken place. It seems that the roebuck's major task is now accomplished, yet the sister still honors the connection to her roe-brother.

There are many variations as to how a wounding can occur in the brother-sister relationship. In the Japanese tale "White Bird Sister," a wicked stepmother kills the sister so that her own daughter can marry the sister's bridegroom. The bridegroom is introduced into the story at the same time that the stepmother replaces the sister with a false bride, thus merging these two events. This differs from "Brother and Sister," where these two movements occur separately, with some recovery time in between. In "White Bird Sister," the brother, who has witnessed his sister's murder by their stepmother, is then forced to become a servant to the false bride. Meanwhile, the sister's spirit returns as a white bird. She speaks with her brother for several days, helping him adjust to this new household in various ways. Finally, feeling helpless in the face of his sister's imminent departure into the spirit world, her brother brings the bridegroom to her. The bridegroom, a Lord, redeems the sister from her bird form and marries her. The false bride and her mother are killed, and brother marries a suitable bride.

"White Bird Sister" shares many motifs with "Brother and Sister": a jealous stepmother, a false sister (wife) who is the stepmother's own daughter, brother bringing the bridegroom to his sister, and the bridegroom's pivotal role in reversing the sister's fate. However, in "White Bird Sister," brother is passive and weak as an animus figure. The negative mother, who brings about the wound, is a powerful killer, and brother is no match for her. Unlike the brother of "Brother and Sister," he does not take the initiative early on and escape from the life-denying environment with his sister. When he does leave, it is in service to the false sister, the shadow side of his sister.

The true sister in the Japanese story is the stronger one of the pair, and as a bird-spirit she directs the brother's actions. Only when the brother and the bridegroom-Lord team up can sister be saved. The Lord provides the vitality that brother lacks.

The sister is directly wounded by the negative mother-complex; on the surface, she is "possessed" by her shadow—the false bride. Psychologically, the murderous nature of the would-be-nurturer (as "mother") destroys what ego strength this young woman had. The brother-animus becomes enslaved to this shadow as well, so that the girl's faith in her life is nearly wiped out. The shadow, or dark unacceptable side of the girl's personality, dominates her conscious life, and her soulful nature is trapped in the body of a fragile white bird. The only hope is that the Lord, who is the positive masculine figure, will perceive what is happening and redeem the sister's true self.

Sometimes a woman appears to be living out her dark, negative, unpleasant side. For some time, she may live the life of the "false bride," not even aware that the true bride is still alive in her. She becomes cynical and negative, and this cynicism enslaves her brother-animus also. Deep inside, the true bride longs for relationship with the brother and the lover, but the woman remains unaware of that longing. The somewhat fragile hope for this woman is that in time the right "person" will come along who can see the white bird within her. If possession by the negative mother is strong enough, most likely the right person needs to be an outer figure, because the internal Lord may be too deeply buried in the unconscious. The Lord (the idealized masculine principle) will then be projected onto that person, and through relationship with him the woman can come to "know herself" again. She will feel a stirring of "who she once was" (the young sister who had the potential to become a healthy woman) and realize she wants to recover her life. Once the sister becomes conscious of these aspects, the dark and negative side of her personality is put in its place, in the unconscious, and a balance of conscious and unconscious can be achieved.

A client of mine, now in her forties, had lived many years of her adult life caught in cynical "possession" by the "false bride." As children, she and her siblings were abused by their father, and their mother was emotionally unavailable to them. As she grew up, she developed an eating disorder—but spoke of this weakness with no one—and lived a "strong, tough woman" lifestyle. In her twenties she became attached to a man with whom she shared a "buck-the-system" camaraderie.

When she entered analysis, she wanted very badly to understand what was going on in the unconscious. She had an inkling of the "true sister's" existence within herself. Her dreams were of male junkies controlling her. Then she had a dream of her father's death. In this dream, her mother was very unlike the dreamer's actual mother; this dream mother spoke as though she "knew" something, and said, "It is the boys we need." The boys were the dreamer's two brothers who had been with the father in the dream when he died.

Around the time that she had this dream, this woman began thinking about the one brother with whom she felt a strong alliance. He was someone she could always talk to, unlike the man with whom she lived. She began to acknowledge to herself a dissatisfaction with her tough woman exterior and with the relationships that encouraged it. She felt weak and vulnerable, afraid to face all of this, but realized she had to in order to truly know herself. It is the true bride, covered up by years of toughness and cynicism, with whom this woman is now becoming acquainted. The inner brother can help her in uncovering that part of herself. This life story and the tale, "White Bird Sister," illustrate other ways in which the brother-sister bond experiences wounding, usually from the outside world.

In "Brother and Sister," wounding occurs in two movements. The first takes place when the brother and sister's safe world in the forest is invaded by the outside world—when the King and his huntsmen arrive. This is followed by another period of "time passing in peace and harmony," as the sister, now married to the King, lives with him and her roe-brother in the palace. As during the earlier time in the forest, the psychological picture is one of apparent balance between the conscious and unconscious realms. These balances are necessary as "resting spots" after psychological upheaval. They provide a time for reorganization, and if we are conscious, perhaps even preparation for the next battle.

We all know these times of balance. Looking back over one's life, it is easy to say, "I felt so satisfied/peaceful/sure of myself then. Little did I know that I still had so much to learn." This is the position of balance that sister and her enchanted brother enjoy at this point in the tale. The balance is temporary and somewhat precarious because the sister has thus far developed more of a connection to her own masculine nature than to the feminine. She is a beautiful maiden when the King marries her, but her feminine development still has a long way to go before she earns the title she now carries of "queen."

Specifically, the sister gave up mothering, a psychological and emotional area of her feminine being, early in her journey in order to find a new way of being with her brother-animus. She and her brother both "cared for" each other—he took her by the hand, she took care of him (when he allowed it!) as a young roebuck—but the realm of mothering has essentially been left behind by the pair. The danger now is that she might act out a false (negative) mother role with the roe-brother, whose activity in the tale (and in the woman's early development) is now over. She might hold him to her as an undeveloped experience of the bond, living in an immature and dependent relationship to the world around her. She is elevated as a queen, but he is still a roebuck, now only playing in a palace garden. If the brother imago is to continue making itself more fully known in the woman's psychic development, he will soon need to regain his human form. A connection between the mother archetype in the psyche and the sister's own feminine being will need to occur before the wounding stage is complete.

This is a powerful point in the tale, and it is a powerful experience in a woman's life. She is standing near a precipice, and the danger is not just to the brother realm, but also to her psychological life as a whole. She will now need the faith it takes to *live* what she has intuited before: the meaningful connection between her inner experience and the world around her.[7] That meaningful connection can serve her next transformation. It is her only hope.

2. THE MOTHER RETURNS

Feminine development requires working with the inner image and experience of "mother." This is a psychological reality for men and women. Fairy tales and myths verify this reality. Fairy tales provide images of *how* this work may occur in various psychological patterns. In "Brother and Sister," the sister leaves the mother in the beginning of the tale, and she must "go back to" the mother before her story can conclude. The sister has married the King, yet this feminine development (becoming a woman and wife) has occurred without an active involvement on her part. This is the pattern in the brother-sister tales where the sister marries before the healing/redemption stage has begun. The king asks her to marry him, and she simply acquiesces. There is no particular joy or involvement. This is because the sister is not yet grounded in her feminine identity. She is not safe or secure in relation to her own body. The grounding and connection will come when she can *say who she is*. In tales such as "The Twelve Brothers" (discussed in Chapter 16), the sister is actually instructed to remain "dumb" during her entire marriage until her brothers are redeemed from their raven form. Then, when the tale concludes (and the healing/ redemption phase has occurred), she regains her voice and tells the King who she truly is.

This is just what happens in the psychological development of a brother's sister. She may have difficulty in developing her own masculine strength beyond the brother realm, or she may not see the need to do so because brother relationships and brother energy serve her so well. However, her greatest challenge and greatest peril lie, not in further masculine development, but in the feminine realm, where she feels absolutely powerless in the face of the Great Mother archetype.

---

[7] Remember her words at the beginning of the story as she and her brother are leaving home: "Heaven and our hearts are weeping together."

The hardest task that the sister-Queen must face in the wounding stage is her re-encounter with the witch-mother. Even during the period of peace and harmony at the palace, this dark feminine power is beginning to make itself known. It is waiting in the unconscious for the right time to enter consciousness. When the sister-Queen gives birth, becoming a mother herself, she can no longer abandon mothering to the dark realm of the psyche. She must connect with positive mothering, and that requires facing the negative mother as well. The birth is the "right time" chosen by the witch-mother to re-enter her stepdaughter's life. The sister faces a deathly challenge in order to learn about this side of herself. She will now either cultivate her own relationship to mothering or fall victim to the negative mother.

Emotionally, a brother's sister is a woman who is most comfortable in the company of men. Her relationship to her own feminine nature is often blocked by a negative mother-complex. At a very basic level, she cannot tend to her own life. Women in this complex have turned away from learning about "feminine ways" in favor of the brother-sister bond. This block will not always be obvious because the woman may appear flirtatious (a "feminine" characteristic), solicitous, or even seductive towards men. In other words, she may seem feminine by society's standards. It is most often the feminine characteristics associated with mothering, particularly her ability to love, nurture, and attend to *herself*, that are wounded.

Jung's work with the negative mother-complex is helpful in interpreting this problem, which is the theme of the next developments in the tale:

> The woman with this type of mother-complex probably has the best chance of all to make her marriage an outstanding success during the second half of life. But this is true only if she succeeds in overcoming the hell of "nothing but femininity," the chaos of the maternal womb, which is her greatest danger because of her negative complex. As we know, a complex can be really overcome only if it is lived out to the full. In other words, if we are to develop further we have to draw to us and drink down to the very dregs what, because of our complexes, we have held at a distance.[8]

---

[8] *CW* 9i § 184.

When the sister-Queen gives birth (facing the "chaos of the maternal womb"), her husband, the King, is away hunting. The sister-Queen's masculine protection is not available to her precisely at the time when she performs this most feminine of tasks. Her brother apparently cannot help her either, so she faces the experience without animus defenses.

What ensues is a long-overdue feminine struggle. The sister-Queen now steps out of her Artemis role and her identification with the brother-animus. As she becomes a mother, she moves into a much less secure feminine country. As Jung suggests (in the above quote), to move forward in her development, she must "drink down to the very dregs" her negative mother-complex.

What is the connection between the sister-Queen and her witch stepmother? The sister-Queen must come to terms with her or she will always be "at her mercy." These two share a feminine connection to the world of nature and a strong medial ability. From early in the tale, the sister has had an (intuitive) ability to experience the world through more than the five senses. She "sees" heaven sharing in her and her brother's tears, and she "hears" the messages of the brooks. The stepmother is also accomplished in the arts of magic, but it is black magic. However, of the two, only the negative mother has held the key to the feminine power of transformation until this part of the story. In this final struggle, the sister experiences the mother's dark magical power and her own connection to it. She can now also participate in transformation. She is able to see that dark magical power is only one expression of the archetypal feminine.[9] Why could the sister not see this earlier?

When very young, the sister experienced a split in the archetypal energy of the Great Mother. This split is common in fairy tales, and therefore we know that it is common in the life of the psyche. Her "good mother" died and was replaced by a witch. Even given the strengths the sister-Queen has acquired at this later point in the tale (connection to nature, Artemis spirit and link to the roebuck, marriage to the King), her feminine nature is vague and often weak or reticent.

---

[9] Similarly, in "Prince Danila Govorila" discussed in the preceding chapter, the sister brought new meaning to the ring's power. The witch had used it to enslave brother and sister, "marrying them" to her regressive purposes, but the sister journeyed to the underworld and brought her brother another bride.

There is little energy in it. *She* did not want a drink of water, and *she* did not want contact with the outside world.

Her weakness and fear are symptoms of the split in her feminine nature. The "good mother" is lifeless. The negative mother has all the feminine vitality, while the sister-Queen has yet to explore it. Thus far, she has connected to vitality more safely through strong animus figures, the brother (roebuck) and the King. She has hidden away from the witch-mother, fearing her negative feminine power. This has resulted in a lack of connection to, even a fear of, her own feminine powers.

Then the sister-Queen gives birth. She is "in the fullness of life" as a woman, and this must mean that the negative mother (as part of that fullness) is present also. A woman's defenses become weakened in the moments following the energy-burst of giving birth, and the witch chooses this brief period as the time to arrive on the scene. Her timing is reminiscent of the King's timing during the brief weakening of the roebuck's energy; in both cases, a vulnerability is exposed, and the ego or conscious life of the sister-companion is more susceptible to intrusion.

These moments of undefended weakness are infrequent in the tale, and they are always related to a weakness in the brother-sister connection. Typically, these moments when intrusion might occur are rare. Women with strong bonds to their brothers will usually encounter the negative mother later in life than do many other women, because the brother-sister bond defends against that encounter. Eventually (sometimes not until mid-life) the negative mother finds an opening and sneaks into consciousness.

When the sister-Queen has given birth, the witch-mother becomes a chambermaid in order to deceive her. It is like coming in through the back door, in a humble form to keep the sister-Queen unsuspecting. Chambermaids are characteristically innocuous and lowly figures, or so it would seem. They are female servants in the position of cleaning and caring for bedrooms. Why should the Queen suspect harm, lock her doors, refuse to follow the chambermaid to her bath? This way of tricking the innocent or unsophisticated ego is used time and time again in fairy tales. Snow White, for example, is deceived by her stepmother in the form of an old peddler-woman. How we respond to these figures helps determine what evolves in consciousness. It is important for us to learn that power does not always wear a crown.

The sister-Queen's weakened state and lack of animus defenses have created a time when dangerous elements can enter her consciousness at the most basic level; thus the chambermaid becomes a threat. Further, the sister-Queen needs to develop her feminine nature from the ground up, and the negative-mother chambermaid is a first step. Symbolically, she must learn how to clean up her own room, which really gets into a mess here in the tale. Her "own room" is one way of conceptualizing the sister-Queen's feminine being or feminine space. Her lack of understanding of her own womanly space has caught up with her.

The feminine psyche's own need to know mothering as a part of herself (particularly the psyche of a brother's sister) has brought up the negative mother-complex. If she can't take care of herself, she will die. But this complex is all the sister has ever known in the realm of mothering, and she must "go through it" in order to experience herself as a mother, and more fully as a woman. She will either die or be transformed through such an encounter.

For a woman with a negative mother-complex, the actual experience of giving birth has a difficult and frightening side. I have come to recognize "giving birth" as a metaphor for beginnings and endings. These experiences are ruled by the archetype of the Great Mother, the eternal womb/tomb of our existence.

This fear is very basic and primitive, sometimes even appearing quite mundane. Whenever the woman with a negative mother-complex finds herself feeling and thinking things that she perceives as "bad mothering," this scares her. I found a striking example of this phenomenon in the experience of a client who had had an abortion in her teens. Still haunted by this experience in her mid-30s, she felt she was carrying some dark and evil secret. Neither the fact that many other women she knew had also experienced abortions, nor the fact that she was a child herself when she had the abortion affected her feelings of alienation. The abortion experience fed her negative mother-complex, arresting her feminine development and making her feel that she was a bad and unworthy woman. She could not nurture (mother) herself, because she believed herself to be such a bad person. She had great difficulty facing her own darkness, because this complex told her she would be swallowed by it.

The thoughts and feelings associated with bad mothering may occur in relation to actual mothering, or to some aspect of the woman's psyche that she is unable to nurture, or in relation to other people in her environment. For example, she may on the surface be a "Pollyanna" who wants to see only the good side of herself and those around her. She has great difficulty with her own dark thoughts (we all have them!), feeling guilty and even ashamed of them. As an actual mother, she may concretely attempt to overcompensate for "the mistakes her mother made," consciously attending to her baby's needs and unconsciously neglecting her own, thus inadvertently turning the negative mother-complex against herself. She can't overcome it, and she must eventually get down into it.

Women who have experienced a strong connection to a positive mother figure have indeed learned from their mothers how to nurture and provide emotional sustenance for themselves, for their creations and projects, and for the people close to them. A woman with a negative mother-complex has learned little of this. What's more, a brother's sister has eschewed the company of girls and women. She may have pompously turned her back on womanly ways altogether. The time when a woman gives birth to her first child is a living symbol of powerful transition, and this is when the brother's sister in the tale leaves her distainful attitude behind her. She is on an Inanna-type descent.[10]

In the form of a chambermaid, the negative mother now performs three acts, which, thanks to the sister-Queen's passivity, accomplish the descent and dissolution of the old consciousness pattern (the old sister-Queen). Though a lowly chambermaid, she is powerful. Her three acts are taking the sister-Queen to the bath, replacing her with the one-eyed daughter, and keeping the King away from this false Queen and therefore deceived.

The chambermaid takes the sister-Queen to her bath to kill her. This has been the witch's intention since the sister's childhood. She has arranged for the bath to be hot enough to suffocate the weakened young mother. However, her own words belie her, and reveal another possibility, that of transformation. She says to the sister-Queen, "Come, the bath is ready; it will do you good, and give you fresh strength." Symbolically, the bath is a vessel in which transformation can take place, thus bringing renewal. However, the negativity of the

---

[10] Inanna, a Sumerian Goddess, descends into her sister's underworld realm, dies, decays, and is reborn more powerful than ever as a result.

mother-complex is so overpowering that the sister-Queen, for all practical purposes, experiences the transformation as a death.

The negative mother is powerful, but her flaw is narrow vision. She believes too exclusively in the power of her own spells and magic. This is a truth that all women and men come to know about the negative mother (both internal and external). Earlier in the tale, the stepmother made the mistake of thinking that brother and sister had died in the forest; now, she fails to see beyond the death of the sister-Queen. That this death might be followed by transformation and rebirth does not occur to her because she has a one-sided destructive nature. Neither has it occurred to the sister-Queen. At this point in the tale (as she goes to the bath), the sister-Queen's transformation is imminent, yet she doesn't see it since she is possessed by the negative mother-complex. The negative mother wants to use the bath to destroy. While "[w]ater is that which kills and vivifies,"[11] the negative mother knows only its killing aspect. Negative complexes within us, and people when they are possessed by their negative complexes, exude a powerful life-denying energy.

Here the negative force grips the young mother. Her ego no longer has "control," and she passively goes to the bath allowing her breath to be taken away. Losing one's breath, suffocating, is symbolic of a loss of spirit and consciousness. The sister-Queen is left for dead in the bath. It seems she is reliving her own good mother's fate, as though now, in the land of the dead, she has joined her lifeless good mother who had died when she was very young. Only when healing and redemption begin do we see the other transformative side of what has happened.

It is the woman herself, not the "baby" she has just had, that the negative mother attacks. The woman's negative mother-complex is trying to take over her body and have a life of its own. She must face up to the ugliness of this complex in her own personality. Her struggle with it will feel overpowering and leave her "weak as a new mother." The "baby" may look fine, but the woman is suffering.

The chambermaid's second action clearly reveals her purpose as she puts her own true one-eyed daughter in the sister-Queen's bed. The dark mother's daughter is a symbol of that ugliness in the shadow that must be faced. She lies in the very birthing-bed of the new mother,

---

[11] *CW* 16 § 454.

but while the chambermaid disguises her in the shape of the Queen, she still "could not make good the lost eye."

The one-eyed quality links this daughter to the sister-Queen, who can no longer deny her own dark shadow side. The negative mother is narrow minded, only thinking of her own destructive powers, but the sister-Queen also is one-sided. Her "nothing-but" attitude has been subtle, but evident throughout the tale. At the brook she didn't want her brother to drink, and during the hunt she didn't want him to leave the cottage, in both cases because she foresaw doom in his possible actions. She has shown a predilection for the negative outlook in all these situations.

Her one-sidedness has been in part an attempt to avoid the powerful influence of the dark feminine, whether in her stepmother (at the brooks) or in herself (in her avoidance of her own energy through taking a more passive feminine role). Like her stepmother, she has seen only the dark possibilities, the tragic outcomes. She has been blind to the potential power of transformation. Now it seems that she has been led to the very power she has tried to avoid. The sister-Queen is taken over by the witch-mother's power; on the surface, she becomes the one-eyed daughter.

With the sister-Queen dead and the one-eyed daughter in her bed, the chambermaid attempts to deceive the King. The only way she can do this is to keep him away from the one-eyed Queen. Her plan works temporarily. A depression or negative attitude has settled over the whole palace, or "psychic situation." It prevents the King and Queen from coming together. This is reminiscent of the periods in "Snow White"[12] and "Sleeping Beauty,"[13] when all life waits while breath is gone from the positive feminine.

Previously, it has been the brother who has gone out in search of something—the world, water, the hunt—when he felt there was a need for more spirit or energy, but now he is curiously still. This is the sister's battle, and this time he cannot fight it for her. More than the woman does, the male fears the annihilating power of the Great Mother. As a powerful image of "the other," She threatens his very existence. A drawback to the brother-animus, somewhat true of

---

[12] Brothers Grimm, No. 53, pp. 249-258.
[13] Andrew Lang, ed., "The Sleeping Beauty in the Wood," in *The Blue Fairy Book* (New York: Dover Publications, 1965 [1889]), pp. 54-63.

all animus energy, is that it often protects the sister from her own feminine nature. She has to go through this struggle on her own. When the sister-Queen dies, her previous over-identification with the brother-animus dies too. This must happen for the inner *brother-sister pair* to become more powerful.

The time of conscious possession by the negative mother-complex is a highly significant time for a brother's sister. For once her brother cannot assist her; in fact, his assistance is what she *does not* need, and yet it is essential to her psychological well-being that she not lose her connection to him. The roe-brother is a symbolic carrier of her earliest feelings of wholeness and union. Were she to lose faith in the brother-sister relationship, it would be a losing of faith in all that her life has meant up to this point. In the tale, no matter how great the peril, the sister remembers her brother.

3. RECOGNIZING THE WOUND

The wound ushers a young brother's sister into an experience of the world around her. Leaving the safety of the warm, unconscious bond with her brother, she must make other connections, form other relationships, and grow up. During this time, she will come up against her own feminine deficits, and that experience will eventually push her to do some difficult soul-work for the sake of her own womanhood.

Her wound also leads the sister into her own individuation process. That process is the psychic parallel of growing up and aging; it is a process of "maturation, unfolding, and rounding out of the personality,"[14] through turning back to the unconscious for deeper knowledge. This usually begins in the second half of life, but no matter when it begins, it is the recognition of the brother-sister wound that often turns a sister's gaze back toward the realm of the unconscious. This is a necessary step toward the conscious process of healing and redemption, which results in the sister's psychological transformation.

---

[14] Jolande Jacobi, *The Psychology of C.G. Jung* (London: Yale University Press, 1973 [1942]), p. 107.

CHAPTER SEVEN

Healing/Redemption: Feminine Wholeness and the End of Enchantment

When a brother's sister has turned inward, recognizing her wounded feminine self and her wounded brother-animus, images of healing and redemption begin to arise. This is where the woman outgrows the negative mother-complex. That complex has kept her from doing what she had the capacity, but not the wisdom, to do all along: to become a more complete woman and to free her brother from the curse of enchantment.

A client of mine who had struggled for years with self-doubt frequently dreamed of her dead hero-brother. This brother had committed suicide in early adulthood during a manic phase of a severe bipolar disorder. Before the onset of his mental illness, he had been a strong and heroic figure for this woman. In recurring dreams, he came to visit her and then wandered off again. The dreams left her with a sense of his powerful influence over her, an influence she could "do nothing with" because he was gone physically. She felt controlled by "him," yet without the support and encouragement he once gave her. His suicide had robbed her of that, and she felt unable to provide for herself in the ways that once he had provided for her. She lived with the painful awareness of these feelings for over twenty-five years, recognizing how wounded she was by his death.

Entering analysis in her fifties, twenty-seven years after her brother's death, she had a new kind of dream about him:

I am sitting with my brother John. We are talking about his daughter and the problems she's having. They seem to be related to school (college), or something like that. He keeps making these chauvinistic statements about what she should do. It's all about rules and he seems like some big authority. Finally I say, "No, John, you are wrong. A lot has changed since you were here, and young women are freer now."

My client believed this was an important dream, because she had some power and wasn't just controlled by the image of her brother. In fact, the dream reveals the beginning of a redemption process. After her actual brother died, this woman had felt "helpless," unable to withdraw her hero-projection from him. Like the sister-Queen, she had no positive feminine strength to draw upon, and her recurring dreams reflected an unfulfilled longing, an unrequited hope for contact. She was a wounded sister longing for the bond.

The new dream indicated a freeing of her own feminine nature (and also perhaps the brother-animus) from that wound. This wound had rendered her powerless in the face of animus strength "out there" (she projected the hero and strength onto men). The dream showed the possibility of forming a connection to an inner feminine strength that could simply say, "This is the way it is." For this woman, feminine healing is needed in order to relate to the inner brother-animus as an equal and companion, rather than as the unreachable hero. This kind of relating happens in the dream.

This healing of the feminine is what begins to occur in "Brother and Sister," after the sister-Queen has been suffocated in the bath by her stepmother. While the conscious world is at a standstill, activity slowly begins to take place below the surface.

The sister-Queen has been left for dead in the bath, and the one-eyed daughter has taken her place. The negative mother has managed to kill and replace the sister-Queen, just as the sister-Queen's own positive mother had died and been replaced by the stepmother. It might seem that the woman, the sister-Queen, is caught in the same trap as her mother before her. But that is not the end of the story. This is where the mystery begins to occur.

In death, the sister-Queen connects to her own positive mother *who has been dead inside her all these years.* The laborious and still treacherous ascent from the underworld begins as the sister-Queen resurrects her own inner mother. That is what is happening while she makes her nocturnal visits to her child and brother. Now, for the first time, she is truly experiencing personal suffering, free of the neurotic obsessiveness that passed for suffering when she was possessed by the negative mother-complex.[1] In her ghostly form, she suffers not just for herself but for her own mother as well. All women are united in this struggle. It is an archetypal struggle that is absolutely necessary for women of our time. Whether the wounding comes from individual mother-daughter relationships or from cultural wounding of the feminine, a "mother's suffering" is what is needed to heal this deep wound to our feminine nature. This kind of mother's suffering can be experienced, as one friend shared with me, in the process of working on and "giving birth to" a project or creative venture, as well as in the concrete experience of bringing a child into the world. In many ways, we are capable of loving someone or something as a mother loves her child; in that profound love, we simultaneously experience suffering and healing, and our feminine being is made whole.

For the third time in the tale, "some time passes," and in that time three figures are present during the sister-Queen's visits: the nurse, the baby, and the roe.

The nurse provides a conscious response to the unconscious ("dead") presence of the ghostly Queen. It is as though she "keeps tabs" on the unconscious proceedings, watching but telling no one. She is an image of healing, an art the sister had begun to learn when she was using herbs to heal her roe-brother's foot. This nurse also is able to take in and hold, without immediately reacting to, what she sees in the natural world, an ability she shares with the sister-Queen. In the image of the nurse, feminine traits that the sister was developing all along unconsciously begin to emerge, and it is this mature receptive feminine figure who keeps watch over the sister-Queen and her family. The sister's femininity is getting ready to come out of hiding.

When I say the "sister's femininity," I am referring to the individual's own unique expression of her feminine nature. This is a combination of various developing feminine traits that have appeared

---

[1] This would be all the pain that stemmed from activity related to her one-sided narrow vision (the "one-eyed daughter")—trying to hold her brother back from the brooks and the hunt, thereby staying stuck in a regressive pattern, and finally going passively to the suffocating bath with the disguised witch.

throughout the tale, but have not—before now—"gelled" in the sister's personality. Such characteristics as the sister's loyalty, her Artemis authority and healing ability, and her original keen connection to the natural world are all in the process of transforming and coming together during this phase of the tale.

The nurse archetype is a significant aspect of the feminine principle, diminished in our modern attitudes to "doctor's helper," but carrying an ancient connection to the divine. In ancient times, temple priestesses were trained to be practitioners of the healing arts as well.[2] So the nurse is able to experience a mystery, and act in a mediating (priestess) role between the conscious world and the realm of the dead where the sister-Queen finds herself.[3]

The nurse is the chambermaid's nemesis. They are on opposite ends of a pole. The negative mother chambermaid is caught in the material world, unable to witness or even imagine the mystery of transformation that is taking place. The nurse as healer and priestess is able to witness and gauge the proper moment for action. Whereas the chambermaid has tried to keep the King in the dark about what has happened to his wife, the nurse brings the King to the scene at the right time for him to assist in his wife's rejuvenation.

The sister-Queen gave birth to a baby boy prior to her death. On the surface this may look like just one more masculine figure in the life of a woman who already surrounds herself with men. However, there is something unique and symbolically powerful in a woman giving birth to a boy-child. The baby is a creation *out of her own feminine body*, not out of the mother-complex nor out of the male-dominated environment in which she dwells. He is an image of a dawning (phallic) creative awareness that is all her own. Unlike the masculine energy that a father, or even a brother, may provide and impart to a woman, her son brings her the experience of *giving birth to* masculine potential. Symbolically, this furthers her independence.

The son is also proof that she has a feminine body, for it takes a woman's body to give birth. Of course, this idea sounds extremely simplistic, yet this proof is critically necessary in order for a brother's

---

[2] Barbara G. Walker, *The Woman's Encyclopedia of Myths and Secrets* (San Francisco, CA: Harper & Row, 1983), p. 731.
[3] The masculine counterpart to this nurse figure is the huntsman, who mediated between the roe-brother and the King earlier in the tale.

sister to finally step into her feminine body. "He" had to be born for the sister-Queen to make her descent. Now the baby provides a vital connection for her to the world of the living.

"He" may symbolize her newfound ability to speak up for herself, take a stand of her own, or to bring her work into the world. He may also be born when a woman literally gives birth to a boy-child. An alchemical process is at work in the woman when a boy-child is born, symbolically or literally. She is participating in the creation of her own masculine potential. Here, in our story, the sister nurses her boy-child, keeping him from the contamination of her one-eyed shadow.

The sister-Queen's other connection to the world of the living at this time is her roe-brother. She pets him when she comes to nurse the baby. Her brother is the masculine half of the sister's inner Self-image, a symbol of the meaning and strength of who she once was and who she will be again. In petting him, she is maintaining their bond of love.

Throughout the bonding and wounding stages, there are two feminine experiences, related but never touching, in a brother's sister. They are the experience of the negative mother and the experience of the hidden suffering woman, biding her time. The latter is the dead positive mother, alluded to at the beginning of this tale. She is carried by a brother's sister, though the woman is rarely conscious of this inner figure. I have heard many women speak of coming to a new awareness of their mother. They realize that what they had previously experienced as negative was a woman who had been forced to abandon her own life. "She" has already shown her presence within the sister in this tale. She is the deep, knowing side in the sister's tendency to "stay," when the brother tends to "go."

This deep feminine way of being is ultimately the salvation of the sister-Queen. The negative mother said, "Die," yet she stayed, albeit only as a ghostly presence. She remained present to her boy-child, to her roe-brother, and also under the keen observation of the night nurse.

The negative mother is so caught up in her own power that she refuses to suffer. For example, in this tale she seeks to punish and even kill the brother and sister instead of suffering her loss of the children. In her own way, the young brother's sister had also resisted suffering when she begged her brother not to drink from the brooks and not to go to the hunt. When finally that other inner woman (the good mother, who has been "dead" but awaiting revival) is acknowledged, the negative mother no longer has power over the brother's sister. Her redemption is complete when the King—the fourth and last witness to her ghostly visits—speaks the simple truth of what he has observed, affirming that she is none other than his wife.

This section of the tale portrays a deeply mysterious time for a brother's sister. It is the most chilling part of the tale because she loses her life and exists only in a ghostly form. Yet in that very loss of life the sister-Queen recognizes herself and steps into her identity. In actual life, and in the eyes of ordinary consciousness, the mystery of this time may go unnoticed. One brother's sister now in her mid-forties had a child in her early thirties. This was a difficult time for her, as she was in a marriage that was physically abusive. She had been unable to gather the courage to leave the marriage, and in fact didn't find that courage until the baby was two years old. Meanwhile, her connection to her baby was strong. She felt sure of herself—of her love, her decisions, and her effectiveness with her child. In that relationship she experienced a newfound sense of vitality.

When this woman did leave the marriage, that very mothering vitality helped her go out on her own. She was not just leaving a physically dangerous situation; she was leaving a psychological entrapment as well. During the marriage, her own life-denying feminine side, her unacknowledged shadow, was in league with the negative animus, which was lived out in her husband. Yet, with the birth of her baby, a new feminine energy was "born" as well, and the time that energy needed to take hold in consciousness (two years) was like the time of the sister-Queen's nocturnal visits in "Brother and Sister." Finally she wanted to "mother" herself with the same energy she had given her baby. Like the sister-Queen, this woman was finally able to acknowledge who she was and bring her more whole feminine being out into the world.

After she left her destructive marriage, she began to make plans for entering a profession she had long wanted to pursue. She opened up to possibilities that she had previously felt were unattainable. At this time, she had a dream in which her brother had also entered into this profession. Simultaneously, she began to have spontaneous memories of her actual early relationship with her brother, and what came to her repeatedly was how this brother had believed that she could "do anything that she set her mind to." He had encouraged her individuality when the two of them were little children.

Such spontaneous memories are of symbolic importance, carrying a message from the unconscious. The woman's memories represented what was coming into her consciousness, an energy for which "brother" was the best image. The brother image carried her back to her origins, and she found that her early relationship with him held the seeds of the "flowering" she was now experiencing. This brother's sister story illustrates what happens imaginally in the latter portion of the fairy tale. The sister gradually connects to her feminine roots, becoming a more whole woman, and then her roe-brother can become "human" again.

In the last sentence of the tale, the brother regains his human form. Sister and brother have both undergone a transformation. They have been redeemed, she from death and he from his roebuck form.

During most of the tale, the brother was a roebuck, symbol of the sister's own inner brother potential. His animal form intensified their bond *and* (paradoxically) intensified their need to reach beyond that bond. While the sister lived with him, the animal form kept the brother-animus camouflaged (not a "real" brother to the outside world). Through intimate contact with the roebuck, the sister has learned how to "be" in the "forest:" wary, sure of foot, still when necessary, and ready to act when the need arises. This way of being has served her in her feminine transformation process. The roebuck is connected to the evolving "questing spirit" of the brother's sister. Also, she has learned to harness and lead the roe-brother, which connects her at a very deep level with her own Artemis nature. The sister-Queen's energy and creative drive, in the form of the roebuck, sometimes served her well, at other times it controlled and pushed her into involvement in the world, but finally it had to be transformed again.

The witch-mother is the dangerous force that gave the brother his roebuck energy, and her cloaked power over him (the enchantment) is now at an end. It is at an end precisely because the sister-Queen has finally "opened her other eye" and acknowledged the feminine energy in the psyche. With feminine grounding, she will no longer need to keep a leash on her creative energy. The final step in the healing/redemption stage for a brother's sister is to move out into life, with the brother-sister pair as an inner symbol of the underlying potential in all human relatedness: a union in equality of hostile yet loving opposites.

PART THREE

The Brother's Work

CHAPTER EIGHT

The Story: "The Death of Koshchei the Deathless"

The brother-sister relationship presents a man with a unique and psychologically enriching journey, just as it does a woman. He may start to recognize the inner dynamics of the brother-sister bond early in life, through a relationship with an actual sister, cousin, or friend. Or this recognition may take place in adulthood, through a "revelation" in which he sees a new way to relate to women, ultimately opening the inner channel that connects him to the sister within.

Our culture encourages a very limited relationship between men and women, and this cultural deficit also serves to restrict the development of our inner relationship between the masculine and feminine principles. Women and men alike are becoming aware of the subtle (and blatant!) negative effects of adhering to these cultural restrictions. For women, adherence to cultural images of the feminine can lead to a loss of voice, depression, anorexia. Clinically, what we call "borderline tendencies" in women are often a result of the woman's early experience of severe external limits being placed on her efforts to find her own identity and voice.

Similarly, antisocial tendencies that are becoming more and more prevalent in men of our time can be seen in relation to severe early limits being set on what a man can expect to do and be in his life. These limits particularly restrict a man's access to his own inner feminine qualities, which Jung called the anima. The cultural result: a loss of soul, leading to destruction and violence. Or at least the appearance of loss of soul. Nothing is truly lost in the psyche, for all that goes underground into the unconscious can rise again. Through connection to the inner sister, men can begin their own transformation, leading to a reconnection to, and rejuvenation of, the experience of the Self, that divine energy in human spirit.

A tale which beautifully, and sometimes graphically, depicts the perilous brother's journey is the Russian fairy tale, "The Death of Koshchei the Deathless." Here is how the tale goes:

* * * * *

"The Death of Koshchei the Deathless"

Once in a certain kingdom lived Prince Ivan, who had three sisters. They were Princess Marya, Princess Olga, and Princess Anna. When his parents were lying at the point of death, they said to their son, "Give your sisters in marriage to the first suitors who come to woo them. Don't keep them by you."

After the parents died and Prince Ivan buried them, he went strolling with his sisters in the green garden to solace his grief. Suddenly the sky grew black and a terrible storm came up.

The prince quickly took his sisters home, and no sooner had they got into the palace, than thunder pealed, the ceiling split open, and into the room came flying a falcon bright. He smote upon the ground, became a brave youth, and said: "Hail Prince Ivan. Before I came as a guest, now I come as a wooer. I wish to propose to your sister, Princess Marya."

"If my sister finds you to her liking, I will not interfere. She may marry you, in God's name."

The Princess Marya consented. They were married, and the Falcon bore her away into his realm.

A whole year went by, and one day Prince Ivan and his two sisters went to stroll in the green garden. Again a storm cloud arose, with thunder and lightning.

Prince Ivan quickly took his sisters home, and when they entered the palace the thunder crashed, the roof burst into a blaze, the ceiling split, and in flew an eagle. He smote the ground and turned into a brave youth, who spoke:

"Hail Prince Ivan. Before I came as a guest, now I come as a wooer. I wish for the hand of the Princess Olga."

Prince Ivan replied, "If you find favor in her eyes, then let Princess Olga marry you. I will not interfere with her freedom of choice."

Princess Olga consented and married the Eagle. He then carried her to his own kingdom.

Another year went by, and Prince Ivan said to his youngest sister, "Let us go for a stroll in the green garden." As they strolled, a storm cloud arose.

Prince Ivan returned home with his sister, and as they entered the ceiling split open, and in flew a raven. The Raven smote upon the floor and became a brave youth, the handsomest of all. He asked for Princess Anna's hand in the same fashion as the other two suitors, and Prince Ivan answered, "I won't interfere with my sister's freedom. If you gain her affection, she may marry you."

So Princess Anna married the Raven, and he took her off to his kingdom. Prince Ivan was left alone. A whole year he lived without his sisters; then he grew weary and decided to seek his sisters.

He prepared and set off, then rode and rode, and one day he saw a whole army slain in a field. He called out for any living man to tell him who had slain the mighty host, and one living man said, "The fair Princess Marya Morevna has slain all."

On he rode, and then he came to a white tent, and the Princess Marya Morevna came out to greet him. She asked if he rode of his own will or against his will.

Prince Ivan replied, "Brave youths do not ride against their wills."

At her invitation, Prince Ivan tarried in Princess Marya Morevna's tent, and the two were married. Then Princess Marya Morevna took Prince Ivan to her kingdom.

After some time, the Princess decided to go a-warring, and she gave the housekeeping affairs to Prince Ivan. She told him he could do anything, only he should never look into one closet.

As soon as Marya Morevna was gone, Prince Ivan opened the closet and looked in. There hung Koshchei the Deathless, bound by twelve chains. Koshchei begged Prince Ivan to have pity on him and give him a drink of water. "Ten long years have I been here, with neither food nor water."

Then Prince Ivan brought Koshchei a bucketful of water.

Again he begged for water, saying that one bucket did not quench his thirst. The prince brought a second bucketful of water, and a third time Koshchei asked for more. When he had swallowed the third bucketful of water, Koshchei regained his strength, shook the chains and broke all twelve at once.

Koshchei said, "Thanks, Prince Ivan. Now you will sooner see your own ears than see Marya Morevna again," and he flew out the window in a terrible whirlwind. He came up with Marya Morevna, and he laid hold of her and carried her to his home. Then Prince Ivan wept, and he arrayed himself and set out to look for his princess.

On the third day of his travels, he came to a wondrous palace, and it was the palace of the Falcon and Princess Marya. They greeted him, and his sister asked him to stay. He stayed three days, and then he said, "I must go in search of my wife, Princess Marya Morevna."

The Falcon said, "It will be hard to find her. Leave with us your silver spoon. We will look at it and remember you." He left the spoon and went on his way.

On the third day, he saw an even grander palace, and it was the palace of the Eagle and Princess Olga. They greeted him and asked him to stay. He stayed with his sister and brother-in-law for three days, and then said, "I must go in search of my wife, the fair Princess Marya Morevna."

The Eagle said, "It will be hard for you to find her. Leave with us your silver fork. We will look at it and remember you." He left the fork and went on his way.

On the third day, he saw a palace even grander still, and it was the palace of the Raven and Princess Anna. They greeted him and asked him to stay. He stayed with them for three days, and then said, "I must go in search of my wife, the fair Princess Marya Morevna."

The Raven said, "It will be hard for you to find her. Leave with us your silver snuffbox. We will look at it and remember you." He left the snuffbox and went on his way.

On the third day, he came to where Marya Morevna was. She ran to him, flung her arms around his neck and cried. Then she exclaimed, "Prince Ivan, why did you disobey me and let out Koshchei the Deathless?"

Prince Ivan replied, "Forgive me, and remember not the past; better fly with me and perhaps he won't catch us."

So they fled. When returning home from hunting, Koshchei's good steed stumbled beneath him. He asked, "Why stumblest thou? Scentest some ill?"

The steed replied, "Prince Ivan has come and taken off Marya Morevna."

When Koshchei asked could they catch them, the steed said they could sow wheat, reap and thresh, grind it, eat pies baked from the flour, and still be in time. They galloped off and caught Prince Ivan.

"I will forgive you this time, for your kindness in giving me water. And a second time I will forgive you. But the third time I will cut you to bits."

He took Marya Morevna back to his home. Prince Ivan sat down and wept and wept. Then he returned for Marya Morevna.

As before, Koshchei's steed easily caught Prince Ivan, and Koshchei took her back to his home. Prince Ivan was left alone.

He wept and wept; then he went back for her again.

Marya Morevna protested, saying that Koshchei would cut Prince

Ivan to bits. He said, "Let him do it. I cannot live without you." So they fled together.

When Koshchei caught Prince Ivan, he chopped him into pieces, put them in a barrel, smeared it with pitch and bound it with iron hoops, flinging it into the sea. Then he carried Marya Morevna home.

At that very time, the silver articles at his sisters' homes turned black. "Ah," said they, "the evil is surely accomplished." Then the Eagle went to the sea, caught the barrel, and dragged it ashore. The Falcon flew for the Water of Life, and the Raven flew for the Water of Death.

When the three met, they washed the pieces of Prince Ivan and put them together. The Raven sprinkled them with the Water of Death, and they joined together into a whole body. The Falcon sprinkled them with the Water of Life, and Prince Ivan shuddered and stood up.

His brothers-in-law asked Prince Ivan to come pay them a visit, but he said, "I must go and look for Marya Morevna."

When he found her he told her to find out where Koshchei got his steed. She asked Koshchei, and he told her, "Beyond thrice nine lands, in the thirtieth kingdom, on the other side of the fiery river, there is a Baba Yaga with many good mares. I watched her herds for three days without losing a mare, and she gave me a foal." He showed her his handkerchief which he used to make a bridge over the fiery river. Marya Morevna repeated all this to Prince Ivan, and gave him the handkerchief.

As he traveled, Prince Ivan grew hungry, and three times he was about to get food. First, he thought he would eat one of the chicks of an outlandish bird. The bird said, "Spare my chicks and I'll help you someday." Then, he wanted a honeycomb from a hive of bees. The queen bee said she would return him a favor, if he left the honeycomb. Finally, he wanted to eat a lion cub, and the lioness said she would help him someday if he let the cub live. He went on, hungry as before.

When he came to the hut of the Baba Yaga, she said, "Hail Prince Ivan, have you come of your own accord, or on compulsion?"

He told her he came to earn a steed. Baba Yaga said he could earn one by watching her mares three days, and not losing one. But if he lost even one, she would have his head on a pole.

Prince Ivan agreed to her terms, and each of the three days he lost the mares, wept, and then was helped by one of the animals he had spared. With their help, he succeeded each day.

The Baba Yaga was angry that he was succeeding. But on the third day the bee told him to sneak into Baba Yaga's stable, wait until midnight, and steal away with the sorry colt he found there.

Prince Ivan did as he was told, and he had crossed the fiery river when Baba Yaga came in pursuit. He made it so that she would fall into the fiery river, and she died a cruel death.

Then Prince Ivan fattened the sorry colt, which became an heroic steed, and he went on the steed to Marya Morevna. She ran to him asking, "By what means has God brought you back to life?"

Ivan said, "Thus and thus. Now come with me."

She protested, saying he would be cut to pieces again. But Prince Ivan said that he now had an heroic steed.

This time when Koshchei's steed stumbled, he told Koshchei that Prince Ivan now had a steed better than his. But Koshchei said, "I can't stand it. I will pursue, anyhow."

When Koshchei came in pursuit, the steed kicked him in the head, and Prince Ivan finished him off with his club. He burned Koshchei's body and scattered his ashes to the wind.

Then with Marya Morevna on Koshchei's steed, and Prince Ivan on his own, they went to visit Prince Ivan's sisters and brothers-in-law, the Raven, the Eagle, and the Falcon. Everyone was joyful, and they said, "No wonder you went to so much trouble. Marya Morevna is such a beauty as is rarely found in the world."

They visited and feasted. Afterwards, Prince Ivan and Marya Morevna went off to their own realm.

*****

CHAPTER NINE

Bound to His Sisters

The story, "The Death of Koshchei the Deathless," which is the focus of this section, begins at a different developmental point than "Brother and Sister," the fairy tale discussed in Part Two. It begins with the dying parents' request to the brother that the sisters be married soon. This indicates that the bonding stage of the brother-sister relationship is coming to an end with the sisters' pending marriages, so we must read closely to discover the nature of the brother-sister bonds that have formed so far.

First, we may consider the fact that the brother has more than one sister. This suggests that there is a preponderance of sister energy in his psyche. That there are three sisters, in particular, is also significant. The number three is associated with change, so the sister energy in the brother's psyche may be ready for change. That there are three sisters may also indicate that the man's sister-anima is clearly delineated or differentiated. By this I mean that the young man has developed a connection with three distinct aspects of the sister-anima, and consequently with the brother-sister archetype. What those aspects are becomes clearer when the sisters marry.

Prince Ivan's parents enjoin him not to hold on to his sisters. By implication, we might suspect that he has a tendency to do so. He is content living at home with his sisters. The parents, by encouraging him to find husbands for his sisters right away, suggest that it is time for the bond to experience its first wound. In fact, from the way the next section of the tale goes, it appears that the parents have spoken out of wisdom, since it becomes clear that the sisters could not have developed their full potential, nor could the brother have gone out on his "knightly quest," until they had all left home.

Prince Ivan is the kind of brother who does not easily let go of his sisters. They are his "comfort and consolation." There are men for whom it is difficult to shed the role of brother, particularly that of brother-protector. A contemporary example can by found in the romantic comedy *Benny and Joon*.[1] Benny is a caring brother who lives with his mentally ill sister, Joon. Their parents were killed in a car accident when Benny was an adolescent, and since then Benny has seen Joon as his responsibility. A housekeeper stays with Joon while Benny is at work, but this is fraught with problems because Joon has a terrible temper. At the beginning of the film, the last of Joon's housekeepers has quit, and Benny is at a loss.

Joon is an artistically gifted young woman, who is intelligent, witty, and charming, but volatile when upset. She has been allowed to paint and philosophize at home, but has not moved out into the world as an adult because of her brother's overprotectiveness. Benny is unable to see that Joon has grown into a woman who may be able to live on her own. When she develops a romantic relationship, Benny is forced to face his own life and his own lack of relationships. The brother-sister bond has experienced a wound, and now Benny must learn to relate to himself and to his sister in a new way, with a new energy. Both Benny and Prince Ivan in the fairy tale are in danger of becoming stuck psychologically if they continue in the safe relationships they have with their sisters.

The parents in the fairy tale represent guidance or a ruling principle in the psyche whose power is fading at the tale's outset. They make a dying request, and dying requests are generally considered powerful psychological forces. In fairy tales, the dying word, question, or request often forms the "problem" of the tale. The old order or way of being, represented by the aged parents, needs to be transformed. The problem is how to "honor" the old way of being (that is, grant the request) while still being true to the newly emerging way.

That newly emerging way of being can be found in the brother-sister relationship, and yet the request requires that the bond be severed temporarily. The brother-sister bond must be transformed, and it is that transformation which is the substance of the tale.

---

[1] *Benny and Joon* (1993), dir. Jeremiah S. Chechik.

In *Benny and Joon*, the brother's fierce loyalty to his sister appears to be inextricably linked to the untimely death of their parents. Their death was the equivalent of a request that Benny not break up the family any further. However, in Prince Ivan's case as well as in Benny's the split that occurs leads to a mutual transformation and reconciliation.

It is interesting that in this tale the parental force is not dark or negative. This is unusual for a brother-sister tale. The brother-sister bond, which is indeed strong, has not had to "leave home" or struggle against parental envy, as is often the case.[2] This is a clear example of what Jung called "kinship libido," a desire for original or familial union, to never leave home.[3] Nevertheless, the parents do request that the bond be broken up. Perhaps the request is made out of wisdom.

Each of the sisters' suitors comes to the house to propose in the midst of a tremendous storm, which is also an image of darkness, and each one enters the palace by splitting open the ceiling. This mode of entry shows clearly that Ivan has resisted them. As with the sister in "Brother and Sister," who locked the cottage door against the huntsmen, so Prince Ivan is engaged in the business of keeping his sisters with him and away from potential suitors. The tremendous storm is the clash between his desire to keep his sisters close and the psyche's push to move on to the next stage of development. It takes great force, in the form of ceiling-splitting storms, to get past the resistance and let in the suitors who will win the sisters away.

In the outer world, when a brother attempts to hold his sister back from relationship, she often finally breaks away in an emotionally violent way. We see this in *Benny and Joon*. When Joon tells Benny of her love for the young man Sam, Benny throws Sam out of the house and tells him to never return. Joon and Sam then attempt to run away together, and Joon's struggle with her brother becomes an inner storm

---

[2] In another tale, "The One-Handed Girl" (discussed in Chapter 12), the parents act with poisonous intent to split brother and sister. The parents request that sister and brother each choose their inheritance: They can choose either "blessing" or "property," but not both. The split separates brother and sister at a deep level, and their struggle moves the tale. There is darkness in the psychological workings of our current tale, although it does not come directly from the parents, and we can speculate from Prince Ivan's initial response to Koshchei that he has little or no previous experience of dark or brutal masculinity. It would appear to dwell in his shadow. Prince Ivan's greatest struggle with darkness comes much later, when he has to face the chaos and irrationality of his own desire for union with Marya Morevna. That struggle takes shape in the ongoing confrontations with Koshchei.

[3] We'll examine the pathology of this in Chapter 14.

that drives her into an emotional breakdown. Intrapsychically, Joon can be seen as Benny's sister-anima. She shows us what happens when a man resists developing his own connections to feminine energy beyond the realm of the sister: he is likely to have a ceiling-splitting eruption of psychic content that will force that development.

The connection between brother and sister in "The Death of Koshchei the Deathless" is strong too. Although Prince Ivan "knows" from his own inner parental authority that he should let go of his sisters, he is reluctant to do this and move on to the next stage of development. As long as one of his sisters remains at home, he need not leave. He resists giving up the role of their "protector."

As a brother and sister move toward adulthood, their strongly formed bond creates an illusion of wholeness, family, "enough" completion, so that they erroneously believe that they need not go beyond the confines of the bond. However, the *participation mystique* that the bond creates *must* be dissolved in order for psychological transformation to take place. With each storm in the fairy tale, the complex's resistance is further broken down. While the brother's resistance is evident, he *is* able eventually to let go of the bond because of the wisdom of the parental request and the positive energy of the sisters and their suitors.

Giving up the role of brother-protector is difficult for a sister's brother. In actual relationships, usually it is the sister who finally has to say, "I don't need help from you any more." Both siblings may be sentimentally attached to their old way of relating to each other. The brother may say: "But she doesn't know how to protect herself," while the sister says: "He doesn't even see that I'm taking care of him now." The brother-protector is only one aspect of the brother-sister bond. Since brother and sister are equal, the sister-protector is another of its aspects. In this tale, the sister-protector role is seen in the sisters' bird-husbands, who bring about Prince Ivan's rebirth. The sisters' husbands represent aspects of the brother-hero's masculine nature that he can access only by allowing his inner sister energy to develop.

Perhaps the bond between the brother and his sisters in this fairy tale is so positive and strong that it takes a great tempest, not to mention a little magic, to tear it apart. Each sister marries a suitor who has the power to "break in" to the palace. But also, each suitor is an animal-man, with magical powers. (The importance of their possession of magical powers becomes clearer later in the tale.) Once faced with the suitors, in each instance, Prince Ivan gives in to the inevitable separation. After the ceiling has been rent, the sister's betrothal appears an easy step. This ease parallels that of the sister in "Brother and Sister," when she says "yes" right away to the king's proposal once he has gained entry into the cottage, though she had previously hidden and barred the door to him. In both tales, once the new enters the scene, brother and sister begin to adjust and transform. However, there is more than one sister to deal with in this Russian tale, and once the first sister has been married off, Ivan insulates himself and his remaining sister(s) until the next storm.

A client of mine in his thirties had a dream that he and his sister were separated in a major disaster. In the dream, he said goodbye to her, feeling that this was a good parting, and that they would meet again someday.

In reality, the man was entering a love relationship the likes of which he had never before known, a "major disaster" to the brother-sister bond! He felt devoted to a woman outside of family for the first time. He had not been consciously aware that his bond to his sister was so strong. This was a bittersweet experience for him. He felt both the longing for his new lover and the sorrow of leaving the familial innocence of his life as a son and brother. His dream reflects a dawning resolve to accept separation from his sister, something that Prince Ivan has not yet done at the beginning of the fairy tale. A separation from the sister, a wound to the brother-sister bond, must occur in order for the man to develop his unique personality. The bond maintains an unconscious union with his actual sister and with his sister-anima, which inhibits his psychological growth. At some point, "sister" has to move over, in order to let the brother develop.

Prince Ivan's brother-sister bond undergoes three storms, each separating him from a sister, yet still he is bonded to them. Even after they have married and left, he continues to be in a state of "*participation mystique*" with them. A sister's brother, he is alone yet still linked to his sister-anima.

Some significant masculine development has occurred, however, even though Ivan is still very closely linked to the sister-anima. This masculine development is reflected in the fact that the sisters have all married powerful magicians who were prior guests (friends?) of Ivan's.

By marrying Ivan's sisters, these male figures are now linked to Ivan even more strongly than they were before.

The magic or spiritual power these figures carry often appears in other fairy tales in a different way—as a dangerous outer force that may try to split up the brother-sister pair. For example, in "The Glass Coffin," a powerful magician appears on the scene, who is welcomed by the brother and sister as a guest in their home. Later that evening the magician approaches the sister secretly in her bedchamber and proposes. This angers the sister and she rejects him. She and her brother have prolonged their bond, agreeing never to marry, and desire only to "entertain" the outside world, not to unite with it. The left-out animus in the form of the magician becomes dark and sinister, and strikes both brother and sister. This tale portrays a young brother-sister pair who are happy to have only brother-sister type relationships, and don't develop a psychological capacity for different types of relationships with the opposite sex. They do not allow themselves to know the powerful romantic lure of the non-brother animus or the non-sister anima, and therefore they are unconsciously susceptible to it. The sister organizes her life around her need to have no such encounters, warding off both her own development and that of her brother.

Unconscious areas of the psyche can knock one off balance completely, as is the case in "The Glass Coffin" when the magician finally gets through to the pompous sister. She experiences him as only negative, and the wound to the brother-sister bond eventually comes from the negative animus personified by the magician. The opening or wound through which new energy finally is able to emerge is found in a dream-state induced in the sister by the magician. She dreams of her "redeemer," the honest young tailor who in the end becomes her husband.

In another Russian tale, "Prince Danila Govorila," the brother himself becomes a dark animus figure. He actually behaves like Koshchei, in "The Death of Koshchei the Deathless," by threatening to overpower his sister. He is lured by the promise of a magical lucky ring, given to his mother by a witch who promises him power if he marries the woman whom it fits. Since the ring fits only his sister, he determines to marry her. Sister is miserable at this turn of events, and seeks advice from beggars, who tell her to perform a magic ritual with four dolls. The ritual is effective—it saves her from the marriage bed—

but it also then connects her to a dangerous witch (none other than Baba Yaga) and the witch's daughter, who live underground. The sister and the witch's daughter together outwit and destroy the witch and return to the brother, who is persuaded to marry the witch's daughter because the ring also fits her. He then finds a suitable bridegroom for his sister.

The lucky ring and the witch's promise to give power to the brother if he marries his sister represent a magical union with the unconscious. The ring can lead to a "false union" and an experience of a false self, which is symbolically represented in this tale by the threat of brother-sister incest. It can also lead to a psychologically true union, which is the experience of wholeness symbolized by the four dolls and the four figures at the end (brother-witch's daughter, sister-husband). It is the ring that the brother covets, and too quickly he believes that marriage to his sister is the only means to this end. He is a man possessed by a brother-centered complex or by the sister-anima, which is puffed up out of proportion to other psychic components.

The brother's sister and the sister's brother frequently face the danger of becoming animus- or anima-possessed. An outer-life example is found in the stereotype of the "comrade" in early twentieth-century Soviet Russia, who are sister and brother vis-à-vis the cause and each other. They have no personal feminine or masculine identity. This "type" appears in movies, too, around this time period, and it is a caricature rather than a fully developed character. Such a one-dimensional caricature shows how possession by a complex looks. All individuality is lost with complex possession, because individuality requires an active engagement of one's unique nature and the archetypal energies that are emerging in the personality.

In these two tales, "The Glass Coffin" and "Prince Danila Govorila," the masculine spiritual power is dark and sinister. On the other hand, in "The Death of Koshchei the Deathless," Prince Ivan and his sisters welcome and form an alliance with the threefold masculine power as reflected in the magician/husbands of the three sisters. Even though Prince Ivan himself does not shapeshift by changing from human to animal form as do brothers in many other fairy tales, both he and his sisters are now connected to figures who do have this power. (I shall speak of the specific bird forms that the sisters' husbands take later when discussing Prince Ivan's search for

Marya Morevna.) While this masculine development is important, Ivan is still profoundly connected to his sisters. Further change is called for in the anima realm.

Finally, after a year of being alone, Prince Ivan's weariness drives him out of his palace. Now he is in pain and beginning to recognize that a wound to the bond has occurred, yet he remains true to the old pattern and hopeful that he can re-establish it. Going off in search of his sisters is Prince Ivan's attempt to remain in the brother-sister bond, similar to the actions of the sister in "Brother and Sister," who tried to keep the bond intact by locking the cottage door to keep the huntsmen out.

Nevertheless, when Prince Ivan rides forth to seek his sisters, he exhibits the courage and self-assurance that is typical of one who knows brother-sister union. This is a reminder of the faith in oneself that the brother-sister relationship imparts. Ivan is confident that he can find his sisters, but also confident that he can handle whatever comes his way. It is this confidence that allows him to go into his adventure so freely. The full impact of his wound is yet to come.

Just as a woman with strong internal brother energy will have access to a strength that is not as available to other women, so a man with strong internal sister energy will also have certain advantages over many other men. These are strengths that are directly related to the bond, and the advantage they bring will remain to become internalized as the bond itself transforms into an experience of internal unity. This "advantage" shows up symbolically in two forms during the wounding section of "The Death of Koshchei the Deathless."

First, whenever Prince Ivan loses Princess Marya Morevna (his anima figure), he sits down and weeps before he goes on. Of course, the strength found in crying isn't obvious to many people, particularly in our culture, but in the fairy tales crying is always a good thing. It opens something up and releases something. It prepares one for the next step. Like rain, it fertilizes the earth of our being, making us ready for new growth. But for male figures to cry in fairy tales is rarer than for females, and this is a special quality also for a man in the process of becoming a brave hero. As a sister's brother, Prince Ivan has a profound connection to feeling and to soul, and his ability to access his own tears is an image of that connection. A man who has grown up in close relationship to a sister or sisters possesses this advantage, whether or not his culture recognizes it as such. (In Chapter 18, I will come back to this aspect of brother-development, as I speak of what I call "the questing knight's return.") The inner sister allows a man to maintain connection to his feelings, which guide him in many of life's dangerous undertakings.

The second advantage that a sister's brother has over other men is his connection to the sister-protector. This connection becomes obvious at the end of the wounding section, and leads into the next stage of the man's inner experience of brother-sister union. The silver keepsakes that Ivan leaves with his sisters symbolize the link between brother and sister, and the sister-protection that they provide becomes the restoration of his life. Feminine energy holds the secret of regeneration or transformation from death to life, and Prince Ivan's feminine sister energy is a powerful presence.

During World War II, my mother's favorite brother was stationed overseas. In her letters, she sent him little keepsakes, trinkets really, and he also sent mementos to her. They treasured these little objects that they exchanged during their separation. The keepsakes were worth much more symbolically than their material value would indicate. They were a reminder of the pure and beautiful connection that is possible between brother and sister in the midst of the outer world's harsh reality. In the "The Death of Koshchei the Deathless," the mementos carry this kind of symbolic power, which is realized much later in the story.

These two strengths, the ability to weep and sister-protection, are aspects of the brother-sister bond. They contribute to the brother's sense of faith in his life, which sometimes may look like a "foolhardy" faith, but nevertheless sustains him till he finds the help he needs.

CHAPTER TEN

Wounding

1. THE EMPTY SPACE

Every sister's brother must experience separation from his inner sister to recognize or learn what that sister actually means to him psychologically. Perhaps he has given her too high a position. Like the woman for whom brother is hero, he is a man for whom sister has become soul. He grows weary without the sister's presence, because the soul has gone out of him. Now the wound is beginning to hurt. But as with the wound experienced by the sister in "Brother and Sister," the brother must feel this tear in his bond to his sister for another reason as well—to let new anima energy in.

Prince Ivan finally leaves home, intending to find his sisters, he thinks. But the psyche's journey is under way now, and what he finds is much more complicated than a return to the original bond he had with his sisters.

In the beginning of the tale, Prince Ivan's sisters take up so much psychological space that his dying parents do not even mention the possibility of *his* marrying. Once the sisters have departed and he has felt their absence, a space opens up through which a new kind of anima energy can appear. This space is created by the wound. Prince Ivan is not yet aware of the need for a new kind of anima energy; he just feels weary and empty with a need to find "something." He calls that "something" his sisters; they have provided solace to him in the past, filled his emptiness, and carried his experience of soul.

What Prince Ivan finds when he first rides forth on his journey to find his sisters is a field of slain men, and then the woman who slew them. She is just what he feared, the "reason" he sought solace with his trustworthy sisters. She is a manslayer, a woman warrior, a formidable partner for any man; but the time has come for Ivan to meet her, and the meeting seems "meant to be." The woman warrior is his anima, just as the magicians are animus figures for his sisters. Marya Morevna is somehow fitting as a partner for a sister's brother. Clearly she is dangerous, she embodies his untamed questing spirit, and if he is not careful she may slay him; but Prince Ivan recognizes her as a soulmate right away. The man with a strong sister-anima also has within his psyche the questing spirit potential, and he will be drawn to women capable of living it out. The connection needs to be made conscious so that he can realize this potential in himself rather than simply becoming attached to powerful, driven women and projecting this questing spirit onto them. But such attachments may be a beginning to acquiring consciousness of the questing spirit aspect of his anima, and that is exactly where Prince Ivan finds himself at this point in the tale.

Upon their meeting, Marya Morevna asks the question that a man's anima is likely to ask: "Are you your own man, or do you follow a master?" This is the gist of her question. When Prince Ivan identifies himself as a "brave youth" who follows only his own will, he is speaking more from desire than from deed (what he would like to be true rather than what is really true). He appears to have decided to forget that he was seeking his sisters out of his own heart-weariness. In this decision, the first stage of wounding is completed. He must learn to live up to his proclamation. At this point he speaks out of a newfound desire to "be his own man."

It is often true that in a brother's development, in order to become aware that his anima is more than a sister, a more profound separation from that sister is necessary so that he will feel his own "emptiness." The masculine psyche tends to be more single-minded, whereas the feminine psyche tends to dwell in pluralism more readily (obviously, both prove to be strengths and weaknesses, at different times). In other words, women have more of a natural tendency toward relationship, and they integrate new forms of relationship more readily. For a man, relationship-building is hard work and taxes his single-mindedness. Ivan has learned the importance of relationship through his sisters; now he is about to develop a new capacity in that sphere of his life. So for brother the wound provides an emptying, and then Marya Morevna the warrior woman comes on the scene.

Prince Ivan and Princess Marya Morevna go to her realm, and they are happy until she "gets it in her head to go a-warring." There is a period in which his newfound soul, the new life with Marya Moreva, appears to be all Prince Ivan needs. This is similar to the periods of relative peace and harmony in "Brother and Sister." In this kind of psychic respite, the individual can gather the necessary energy to face the next challenge. This particular respite is destined to be temporary, for the brother has not found his sisters, nor has he fully developed the masculine questing potential that connects him to Marya Morevna. What is more, he has gone to Marya Morevna's realm, meaning that he is still controlled by his anima. In a sense, he has attempted to transfer the control that his sister-anima has had over him to his lover. Paradoxically, it is Prince Ivan's strength *and* his weakness that he can go so readily into the anima's realm.

When a man takes on such an anima, he must be sure not to let her rule him. Prince Ivan is vulnerable to the control of anima energy. He has thus far been ruled by his need for connection to his sisters. He must, in the course of his development, become the "masculine ego" in his domain. This actual position comes later in the tale, when Prince Ivan earns his own heroic steed. But for the time being, he looks more like a puer,[1] with a connection to the feminine dimension of life that makes him a desirable partner, though lacking in focus and in a solid masculine identity.

When Marya Morevna leaves, and Prince Ivan is once more alone in a palace, he finally sees his own shadow. His wife has enjoined him not to open the closet, but this he immediately does, and there he finds Koshchei the Deathless. Unlike the women in tales with this motif ("Blue Beard,"[2] for example), Prince Ivan never hesitates to disregard Marya's request. What is more, in what seems almost an act of masculine camaraderie, he gives Koshchei the water he needs to regain his strength. Of course, this is an unconscious act, in that Ivan doesn't actually know with whom he is dealing.

---

[1] *"Puer aeternus"* means "eternal boy" in Latin. It is a term used in Jungian psychology to signify a man who is more in touch with possibility and adventure than with follow-through and structure. The puer is frequently seen as anima- or mother-bound.

[2] Andrew Lang, "Blue Beard," in *The Blue Fairy Book* (New York: Dover Publcations, 1965 [1889]), pp. 290-295.

Just as the sister-Queen of "Brother and Sister" had to face her dark mother and her shadow, so Prince Ivan must face his shadow, the masculine aggression that would abduct and overpower his soul. Koshchei is Ivan's own dark tendency to literalize and separate from feelings. We saw this tendency at play earlier in the tale, when Ivan proclaimed that he would not stand in the way of his three sisters' wishes, but only after the suitors had to split the ceiling open in order to gain entry! He must learn how to transform this from aggression or dogged resistance into heroic action.

It is through Prince Ivan's act of disobedience toward his anima-woman, Marya Morevna, that he meets Koshchei. The simple act of "disobedience" must occur. Prince Ivan has said he would never stand in the way of his sisters' freedom, and now he has watched Marya Morevna go off "a-warring," without standing in her way. He must, if he is to maintain a relationship to his own anima, get in touch with his masculine strength of will. In other words, he must find his own way of holding her. The act of disobeying Marya is reminiscent of the action taken by the roebuck when his sister wants to hide from the huntsmen. These actions, both internal and external, are highly important in the dynamics between brother and sister (or a sister's brother and his anima). On the one hand, the feminine energy holds a wisdom that benefits the pair; on the other hand, the masculine energy is needed to break out of patterns that are ready to transform. For all her "warring," Marya cannot accomplish this alone.

Prince Ivan's encounters with Koshchei carry the same psychological weight as the sister's dealings with her stepmother in "Brother and Sister." The risk he faces is to his psychological life as a whole, and the fate of his psychic vitality is determined in these encounters. In order to connect safely with vitality, Ivan had formed alliances with his three brothers-in-law, but that was too indirect. He became weary again. Now that he has attached to Marya Morevna, he knows a new and vital anima energy. However, she is proving to be somewhat unwieldy and unavailable. He can't hold her. Through her whimsical nature, she connects him with this dark core of his masculine identity. Now he must find his own relation to masculine vitality and become firmly aware of his own identity, or die in the struggle with Koshchei.

I once worked with a young man who, throughout childhood and adolescence, had lived in a powerfully close bond with his sister. Their bond had not yet gone through its natural transformation, and now he was married to a beautiful and strong-willed woman. While he was interested in working analytically, his wife was keen on controlling that process by letting me know what his issues and weaknesses were, including what she saw as his too-close relationship with his sister. My client's poetic, feeling nature was in a polarized conflict with his wife's desire for rational results. I knew that the most important thing he could do would be to tell her to stay out of his therapy, to "disobey her," while committing himself to his own psychological work. This proved to be nearly impossible for him to do, and he moved to another state before our work had progressed very far, but the young man was clearly in the same struggle Prince Ivan finds himself in at this juncture in the tale.

2. The Deathless Masculine

Disobeying Marya is only a beginning for the young man. His struggles with Koshchei form the second stage of the wounding process. Once he regains his strength, Koshchei's first act is to abduct Marya Morevna and take her off to his realm. At this point, Prince Ivan must grapple with his own penetrating masculine nature, his aggressive and even destructive side. This is an aspect of masculinity that he gave up early in life, in order to be brother to his sisters. He has known harmony, now he must know discord.[3] Koshchei is a dark, earthy (chthonic) masculine "spirit," who seems determined to destroy the union that Prince Ivan and Marya Morevna might enjoy. He is both Ivan's shadow and Marya's negative animus. After all, he is locked in *her* closet.

Must a man separate from the anima, indeed even betray her, in order to find his masculine strength? Perhaps temporarily, but that he must "never see her again" (the words of Koshchei) is a lie. This is the message from the dark side of his own masculine nature, and he must challenge that message, for it expresses the one-sidedness that

---

[3] An interesting note: While Apollo and Artemis are an image of brother and sister maintaining harmony in the heavens, there is another brother-sister pair who embodies war and discord—Ares and Eris. In Russian fairy tales, Koshchei and Baba Yaga are deep, dark masters of the black arts, and they feel more archaic than Ares and Eris.

does not see potential for transformation. We've heard this voice before, in the words of the stepmother of "Brother and Sister." Just as a sister has to face her own inner feminine darkness, so a brother must also face his inner masculine darkness to develop a connection to his unique masculine nature.

It is a testimony to the power of the brother-sister bond that Ivan now reconnects with each of his sisters in turn, as he begins his search for Marya Morevna and Koshchei the Deathless. He will need the psychological presence that they personify in the tasks ahead. This segment of the tale reminds me of a knight's vigil, a gathering of spiritual energy for the road ahead. For the sister's brother, that spiritual energy will emanate from the brother-sister relationship. When Prince Ivan let his sisters go to be married, they each became an even more powerful spiritual presence for him. All three of the bird-princes they marry are symbolic of spiritual strength—the masculine experience of the hunt (falcon), of solar and kingly power (falcon *and* eagle), and of insight into the afterworld (raven). These are masculine traits that a man can integrate via his relationship with the inner sister, and they can now aid the sister's brother in the perilous task at hand. Interestingly, as we so often find in life, it was not by holding on to his sisters that Ivan could connect with these powers, but by letting them go so that they could develop separately from his conscious will.

As he goes from sister to sister, Prince Ivan is establishing a link to the inner worlds they inhabit. It is his lifeline. The sisters and their husbands actually *insist* upon that link, by each asking for a silver keepsake. They know what he does not know about his future, but this knowledge is safe with them. Like good sisters, they use their knowledge to protect his future.[4] This idea of a "knowing" on the part of the sisters and their husbands is borne out later in the story, when they restore Ivan to life with such speed and skill. At this point in the tale, however, they reveal only that they know about Marya Morevna's abduction and that "it will be hard to find her."

The keepsakes are made of silver, a feminine or lunar metal. It can change with the tides, and in Ivan's story it changes with the tides of

---

[4] As the stories in Chapter 12 show, this secret knowledge does not always afford protection. The dark sister may use the knowledge from the unconscious realm against her brother.

his life. Giving the silver keepsakes to his sisters has ensured their spiritual presence with him; they and their powerful birdmen-husbands become guardians of his soul. In the life of a sister's brother, it is all-important for this psychological truth to become an internal reality. This man may cherish his sister, or the sister figure in his life, he may feel protective of her and proud of her, and he may sentimentalize her. It is a daunting task to turn his gaze inward and direct this same loving toward his own feeling and relational life. It defies what our culture tells men they need to be.

After staying with the last sister for three days, Prince Ivan leaves to look for Marya Morevna. His behavior here seems peculiar. He appears to have no plan; he just wants to be with her. We have all heard of the man who would die for love, and here he is. It is a combination of Ivan's puer nature and his sister-anima connection, together with the attraction of this new dimension of the anima reflected in Marya Morevna, that gives him such energy (the *new* attraction is always powerful in the psyche). A sister's brother tends to have a puer nature early in his development, just as the "young" brother's sister tends to appear foolhardy. However, Ivan's lack of a plan has another aspect. On the one hand, Ivan has faith in life and boldly encounters the world; on the other hand, he lacks the capacity to work out a strategy and see it through.

The ability to develop a plan and execute it is locked in his dark masculine shadow. In contrast to Ivan's "perhaps he won't catch us" attitude, Koshchei, Ivan's dark shadow (once he has easily overtaken Ivan and Marya), tells him, in no uncertain terms, exactly what the plan is. Because Ivan has "befriended" this dark shadow side of his own nature in the past (by giving Koshchei the water of life earlier in the story), he is able to buy some time. This befriending of Koshchei is another act of Ivan's that illustrates the brother's faith in his ability to handle whatever comes his way. However, Koshchei proves to be a difficult character to handle, and the brother has to face the masculine qualities he does not accept or know how to use in order to "handle" him. His previous befriending of Koshchei has opened the door for him to reconnect temporarily with Marya Morevna, but only on Koshchei's terms. Even this contact has an inevitable consequence: Ivan will be cut into pieces.

What does this mean psychologically? I believe that Ivan's contact with the deep shadow side of his own personality has created a reaction in his conscious way of being (ego) so strong that this conscious way of being must end. It will be "cut into pieces." That conscious way was the "nice guy" personality, the easygoing companionable man, who is loved by all but now finds himself unable to get and hold onto what he wants. I have known many men, raised with sisters, who had to learn the lesson that Ivan faces with Koshchei. Prince Ivan is going through the motions, seeing Marya Morevna for the three times granted to him, knowing that he must experience the traumatic event foretold to him. So far, he doesn't see a way out of this dilemma. He *must* see Marya Morevna or die trying, and he cannot avoid the consequences of that action. Prince Ivan does not foresee that the ordeal to come might bring about a transformation. At this point, his submission is his most important act. If the sister's brother is ever to integrate something of this willful, powerful masculine energy, he must first allow it to affect him.

There is a parallel between the sister's death in "Brother and Sister" and Prince Ivan's death here. In "Brother and Sister," the sister dies at the hands of a dark feminine power, whereas Prince Ivan dies at the hands of a dark masculine power. They are both "too good" and even naïve in the face of these dark powers, yet the powers at the same time represent their own blind spots. The sister in "Brother and Sister" is smothered to death and Ivan is hewn to pieces. They are opposite forms of death, representing the opposite needs of sister and brother. Whereas the sister needed to recognize her feminine darkness, he must recognize his masculine darkness. It is aggressive, chaotic, and it splits him into a thousand pieces. Most significantly, it splits him off from his feelings (Marya), while also dismembering and disabling his body. When Prince Ivan is killed and dismembered by Koshchei, it is Koshchei who has the upper hand. Psychologically, this might look like a very aggressive and "angry young man." The sister's brother is behaving in a manner that seems totally out of character; gone is the man who was sensitive and open to the feeling side of life. The danger for a sister's brother is that he may become stuck in this angry place. The difficulty in gaining and maintaining a connection to his anima, as well as the separation from his sister-anima, may throw him into an identification with his destructive masculine nature. This can manifest as an outwardly hostile attitude, or as a morose and brooding nature. Either way, the brother's only hope is that the sister-anima has enough consciousness to see the danger and come to his rescue as his consciousness fades.

For example, one sister's brother I knew as a client had so many difficulties in relating to the non-sister anima figures in his life and in developing his own feeling nature beyond the brother-sister bond that a hostile Koshchei way of being became a chaotic sort of refuge for him. At least here, he didn't have to face and deal with his inner suffering, turmoil, and dismemberment. He could do the hewing, rather than being hewn. Fortunately, Koshchei is an archetypal force that is too intense for an individual to identify with without paying a price. And often the price that is exacted can return a man to his "roots," in this case to the positive base from which his life began, the brother-sister relationship. As an older man, he began to pick up the pieces of his life, and, just as with Prince Ivan, those pieces were still there, waiting to have life breathed into them again. For this man, the work of reconnecting to his feeling life, to the love of nature and animals, to the care and attention people need to give to each other, has begun. And that reconnection may be what literally saves his life.

In our fairy tale, once he has been hewn to bits and put back together by the spiritual male/sister-anima forces, Prince Ivan awakes *with a plan.* From here on, he performs as a hero. He has truly awakened a transformed man. Has his death at the hands of Koshchei transferred some of Koshchei's power to him? Now it seems as though Koshchei plays into the hands of Prince Ivan's newfound manhood. After all, Koshchei's tremendous power, like that of the sister-Queen's stepmother in "Brother and Sister," depends upon illusion because he thrives on the fears and inhibitions of Prince Ivan. Just as the sister's transformative feminine energy was trapped in the negative mother-complex (in "Brother and Sister"[5]), Ivan's masculine creative drive in this story was caught in the inner persecutor, Koshchei. The veil that Koshchei and the complexes that spring from his archetypal power throw over perception gives the illusion that there is no other way but to submit to his power. The *other way*, which actually existed all the time, is what Prince Ivan discovers upon his rebirth.

---

[5] See pp. 78-81.

CHAPTER ELEVEN

Reconstruction and Celebration

T he brother's healing process begins precisely when the falcon, eagle, and raven say, "Ah, the evil is surely accomplished." Prince Ivan has finally come to the end of his conscious ability to cope with his shadow problem. He has come to his point of no return. Only now does it become clear that his unconscious support— in the form of the three sister/bird figures—has been laying the groundwork for the next step in the transformation process.

The bird-husbands of Prince Ivan's sisters have a very special significance as aspects of masculine power to which sisters can lead a brother. It seems that birds have a natural connection with the brother-sister relationship, just as do stags (roebucks, deer).[1] Birds in general symbolize a masculine energy that is opposite to the energy of Koshchei, who is literal, destructive, and separates Prince Ivan from his feelings. Birds are lofty, always carrying the ability to "see the big picture." They are the power of spirit and intellect, while Koshchei is the power of brute force and doggedness. If the Koshchei energy uses intellect at all, it is to hack away at life, rather than to contemplate it reflectively. A sister's brother is much more prone to this reflective activity in this thinking, except when he is possessed by his shadow Koshchei's power.

In addition, the raven is a bird who is connected to death and the afterworld, and is known as a messenger from these other realms. He brings Prince Ivan the Water of Death, the first step to rebirth, for it

---

[1] See Chapter 16, on the bird-tales, and my childhood dream discussed in Chapter 3 (pp. 27-28).

makes his body whole again. This is a power which far exceeds Koshchei's status as "the Deathless." Koshchei, by virtue of his name, is unable to transform, while the raven, falcon, and eagle are intimately linked to the powers of transformation. As with the sister in "Brother and Sister," Prince Ivan has had to come face to face with his own destructive, one-sided shadow in order to take the steps toward transformation. Only in his own death can he do this.

The brothers-in-law as birds are enchanted men, but it is an enchantment that they themselves control. As enchanters, they can bring the brother to a new level of understanding or awareness, a new level of relationship to his instinctive core. So at this moment of profound despair, the nadir of Prince Ivan's transformation process, his ability to transcend (the wings of the birds) suddenly bursts forth, and gives him life again.

In this experience, Prince Ivan connects fully to his own "male magic." At this point, the task of this male magic is reconstruction. While the sister-Queen in "Brother and Sister" nurses her baby—a most feminine task, Prince Ivan's bird-power constructs—a most masculine task: it literally puts him back together.

I have said that the feminine principle provides birth and transformation in the cycles of psychological process. Here, the feminine has united with her brother's own ability to soar, to rule, to hunt, and to come back from death. It is no mistake that this appears to be magic. In the course of his development, it is essential for the brother to come to terms with male magic, or the energy of the sorcerer (enchanter). This is the masculine principle in its most spiritual form. The husbands of his sisters provide Prince Ivan with enough male magic to undo what Koshchei's barbaric power has wrought. They are white magic contrasted to his black magic. Through the sisters, whom he can trust, Ivan comes to know masculine powers that he can also trust. The sister's brother often has difficulty with conventional masculinity, just as the brother's sister shuns many feminine pursuits. Still, he needs a positive connection to his own masculinity. In concrete terms this may take place as a man coming to recognize and value his own form of masculine identity, which may manifest in intellectual, artistic, spiritual, or some other less conventional form. I don't want to be so limited as to say a sister's brother *never* develops certain of the more conventional forms of masculine identity, such as those found in sports, hunting, fighting, law-making, law enforcement, the life of the soldier. But typically these will not be the first choices for a sister's brother in terms of his own expression of the masculine principle. He may be an intellectual or poet, like William Wordsworth, for instance, whose relationship with his sister Dorothy was lifelong, and central to him.

As I have said, Prince Ivan awakens with a plan. Now, he possesses the bird-power of thought. Ironically, the first decision he must make is to deny his brothers-in-law's requests to come home with them. Here is the paradox of the brother-sister relationship again. Prince Ivan, and any sister's brother, could get stuck here. The brother-sister relationship does not exist *for its own sake*, but for the sake of the psyche's flow, which is individuation. At least, that is how we humans must relate to the archetypes. Were Prince Ivan to visit his sisters at this point in the tale, he would probably have to be dismembered all over again. It would be regression to allow the brother-sister relationship to satisfy rather than move him.

Prince Ivan has been cut to bits by his own masculine destructiveness, through Koshchei who has a fast steed. Now Ivan realizes that he must earn his own steed—he is claiming the energy that had been locked in his shadow. Through his other feeling-connection, Marya Morevna, he finds out how to acquire a steed, and goes off on this quest. It is interesting to note that Marya helps him here, when he is able to tell her what to do.

In the journey to Baba Yaga's hut, Prince Ivan goes even further into the depths of the unconscious to gain the steed and reclaim energy from the shadow and from the archetypal dark feminine. In order to face Baba Yaga successfully, he must have good instincts and wit. Brute force would get him nowhere. The instinct for self-protection that can come only from the mother realm is supplied by the three "mothers" whom Prince Ivan meets along the way: the bird, queen bee, and lioness. By controlling his impulses, something Koshchei cannot do, Prince Ivan wins these three mother-instincts to his side. They prove more powerful than the one-sided destructiveness of the Baba Yaga.

The Baba Yaga episode in the fairy tale occurs after Prince Ivan has been reborn. His rebirth was an act of finding masculine identity. However, to find and master the steed, an instinctive and earthy energy, he must deal with the mother. Whereas this was a central theme in the sister's tale ("Brother and Sister"), it is less central, though still of consequence, in the brother's tale. Mother rules birth and death, and she must be dealt with for a sister's brother to move freely across the earth. Besides, this particular brother needs lessons in how to protect himself.

The first question that Baba Yaga poses to Ivan is a parallel to the question Marya Morevna had asked upon their meeting. Baba Yaga asks, "Have you come of your own accord, or on compulsion?" When Marya Morevna asked a similar question earlier in the story, Prince Ivan had answered as he wished he were, rather than as he truly was. Now, when asked by a woman who can see through any lies, Prince Ivan is able to answer directly and truthfully. It is an indication of how far he has come in his own development.

In addition to the masculine development that has occurred, the animal mothers whom Prince Ivan has befriended provide a balance to the harshness of Baba Yaga, who is a very destructive and exacting mother. In some tales Baba Yaga can be generous, but even when she gives, she possessively holds on to her gifts. Prince Ivan has *won* the balance provided by the animals. They are truly part of him, since he gave up his own instinctive urges to help them. The sister-Queen in "Brother and Sister" had to give up her life before she could really connect with the inner positive aspect of mothering; Prince Ivan has given up his life for his masculine identity. Now he must give up an aspect of his instinctive survival urges to have an even stronger survival instinct on his side—that of the protective mother. In the course of his journeying, Prince Ivan is continually deepening his relationship to these different components of his anima: the sister, the lover, and the mother.

When Prince Ivan returns to Marya Morevna with his steed, she wonders about the fact that he is alive. This is curious, since it is the second time she has seen him since his rebirth. Was he not fully alive before? The tale does not explain itself here, so we can only surmise that, for whatever reason, it is only now that Marya Morevna recognizes that Prince Ivan is reborn. Perhaps earning the steed was part of his rebirth process. Or perhaps she saw the encounter with Baba Yaga as more life-threatening than his dismemberment by Koshchei. In any event, Marya Morevna at this point in the story finally recognizes that Prince Ivan is truly alive.

Prince Ivan's rebirth cannot be complete until he is reunited with Marya, and that reunion requires that he have a steed as fast as Koshchei's. He has said that he could not live without Marya, and it is evident that Koshchei will stand in his way as long as he can outrun Ivan. From this perspective, Marya's question is fitting. It is an acknowledgement that only *now* in the story can Ivan claim her as his partner again.

When Ivan and Marya have escaped, Koshchei, true to his one-sidedness and doggedness, cannot help but pursue Prince Ivan, even though his steed does not encourage him in the pursuit. Although Prince Ivan has learned how to be versatile in his masculinity, how to shift with the requirements of the moment, Koschei is as myopic as ever. His death is now inevitable. Prince Ivan kills Koshchei, "the Deathless," and thus truly moves into the position of the hero of his own tale.

Fittingly, the last action in the tale is a celebration with Ivan and Marya Morevna, the sisters, and their husbands. They acknowledge that Prince Ivan's efforts were for a worthy cause. Prince Ivan's task has been to free the psyche from the sister-complex and the masculine shadow, allowing the brother-sister archetype to provide soulful energy in his life's journey.

PART FOUR

The Hostile Opposites

CHAPTER TWELVE

Dark Bonds

Not all brother-sister relationships are experienced as a positive or desirable connection. There are many stories of brothers who are cruel or even brutal to their sisters, and of sisters who control and torture their brothers. Or sometimes the brother-sister relationship begins positively but unexpectedly turns dark or difficult. How can we possibly fit these dark relationship stories into the model put forth in this book, which views the image of brother-sister union as creative and transformative?

Yet we must do just that, because negative experiences can be positively transformed and can lead to psychological development just as positive experiences can. Many brothers and sisters have developed profound strength, having worked through the hardships of dark and difficult sibling relationships. Fortunately or unfortunately, it is part of the "human equation"[1] that suffering pulls us down from the heights to which we would soar. That very suffering, if we consider it a valuable experience in itself, can ultimately provide us with even stronger wings to reach greater heights. It is just so with the brother-sister relationships that seem to bring only heartache. In the words of the poet Rilke: "perhaps all the dragons of our lives are princesses who are only waiting to see us once beautiful and brave. Perhaps everything terrible is in its deepest being something helpless that wants help from us."[2] Let us now look to the dragons and terrible stories in an attempt to unlock the wisdom they hold.

---

[1] My source for this expression is "Star Trek: the Next Generation."
[2] Rilke, *Letters to a Young Poet*, p. 69.

1. The Dark Brother: "The One-Handed Girl"[3]

*****

A Swahili tale tells of a family who was quite poor but lived happily for
some time. When the father was near death, he called his son and daughter
to him and said, "Now I will leave you soon. Tell me which you will ask
of me, my property or my blessing." The son said, "Property, certainly."
And the father nodded. But the daughter said, "I want your blessing."
Her father gave her much blessing.

When he died, the family mourned for him as was the custom. Hardly
was the time of mourning over, when the mother fell ill. She called her
children to her and said, "I will leave you soon. Son, choose which you
want: blessing or property?"

He said, "Property, certainly."

But the daughter said she wished for blessing, and her mother gave her
much blessing. Then she died.

After the mourning period, the brother took all the possessions and
left the hut, leaving his sister only a small pot for her corn. But she had
no corn.

Gradually, by lending her pot in exchange for corn, the girl began to
thrive. And she planted pumpkin seeds, which sprang up and produced
many sweet pumpkins.

When the brother heard how the pot had served her, he went back to
the hut and took it from her doorway. But the sister soon was able to
replace the pot, with her earnings from her delicious pumpkins.

Before long the news of her pumpkins spread, so that her brother's wife
one day sent a servant to get some. The girl gave a pumpkin to the servant,
but when he returned the very next day, she had no more ripe ones. The
brother's wife was angry and complained to her husband, lying and saying
that his sister had refused unjustly.

The brother then went to his sister, and in a rage he said he would cut
down the pumpkin vine. She grabbed the vine, saying, "If you cut it you'll
cut off my hand." And the brother cut off the vine and his sister's hand.

The brother then took everything the sister had, and he sold the hut so
that she had no home. The sister bathed and bound her arm carefully,
and went to hide in the forest. She wandered for seven days, and climbed
up high in the creepers for protection.

On the seventh day, she was high in a tree crying. The king's son who
was hunting in the forest, sat under this tree to rest. He felt something
wet falling on him and discovered the beautiful maiden crying in the tree.

---

[3] Andrew Lang, ed., "The One-Handed Girl," in *The Lilac Fairy Book* (New York:
Dover Publications, 1968 [1910]), pp. 185-208.

He asked, "Are you a woman or a spirit of the woods?" When she told him her story, he asked her to come home with him.

The one-handed girl then married the king's son, and they had a baby. Soon the prince was sent on a journey to some of the distant towns of the kingdom, to set things right that had gone wrong. When he had gone, the brother, who now had wasted all his possessions, chanced to come into the town where the king lived. He heard of the prince's one-handed wife, guessed that it was his sister, and a great rage came into his soul. He vowed to ruin her.

The brother then went to the king and convinced him that his daughter-in-law was an evil witch. He asked that she be killed, but instead the king and queen were merciful, and turned her and the baby out of the town.

The poor girl loved her husband, but just now her baby meant so much to her that as long as he was with her, she did not mind anything. She wandered into the forest. When resting, she saw a snake coming toward her, and the snake surprised her by speaking to her. "Please hide me in your pot," he said. So she did, and soon another snake came seeking the first. She said, "He went by, going very quickly."

So the girl saved the snake, and soon he repaid her. He told her to bathe in a certain part of the river with her baby. When she did, her baby fell right into the water. No matter how thoroughly she searched using her one hand, the girl could not find the baby. In desperation, she said to the snake, "What can I do? My baby is gone and I won't ever see him again."

The snake said, "Use the other arm too." Thinking that this was quite useless, because there was no hand to feel with, the girl did what the snake told her. Immediately, she felt something soft and warm, and pulled up her baby, laughing and completely unharmed. The snake had magically restored her hand as well as her baby.

After this, the girl and her baby went to live with the snake and his parents for some time. She felt safe there, and the snakes took good care of her and her baby. She often thought of her husband and wondered how he was.

Meanwhile, the prince had fallen very ill on the furthest border of the kingdom. Kind people who didn't even know him had nursed him. In fact, no one knew where he was. When he was finally well enough, he slowly returned to his home. He found a strange man there, attending the king, and this was his wife's brother. But the king told him that his wife and child were dead. At this, the prince wept and went into mourning.

The girl finally decided to return to her kingdom. She told her friend the snake, and he was sad. But he said, "Yes, it must be. But if my parents offer you a present, only take my father's ring and my mother's casket."

They were small, but magical. The ring would give food, clothing, and even a house, and the casket would set things right if there were danger.

When the girl came near the town, she had the ring build a home for her and her child. It was beautiful, and soon news of the mysterious lady reached the king's ears. So he took his son and ministers, and they went to see who she was.

When she saw them coming, she put on a veil, and she went to greet them with her child. She offered food to the king. As she sat, she recognized her brother among the ministers. "I owe all my misery to him. He has hated me from the start," she thought. But she said nothing, and after the king had eaten, he asked her to tell him who she was.

As she told the story of her life, the king, the prince, and the girl's brother realized who she was. The king felt guilty, the brother wanted to run, but the prince finally cried out, "It is my wife. She is not dead."

Then the girl told the end of the story, saying, "If I hadn't been sent away, I would never have met the snake or got my hand back. So let us be happy and forget all that, for see! Our son is becoming quite a big boy."

She forgave the king, and when asked what should be done with her brother, she said, "Put him out of the town."

*****

the impoverished family: split between property and blessing

That the original family was poor in the beginning of this tale is an important indicator of what is to come. They may have been "happy" (read: in harmonious balance) for some time, but the balance is about to come to an end. Whatever the harmony in the family, it does not have psychic strength or stability. Poor families in fairy tales present us with a situation in which some psychic energy exists in a lowly or undeveloped ("poor") state in the collective psyche. We all know the dark energy of discontent that poverty can breed, and it is frequently expressed in some violent manner. Poverty in the psyche means that there is something within us that is kept down, forced to eke out its existence, even threatened with extinction.

In the tale, the parents in the impoverished family make their children choose between "property" and "blessing," that is, between the material and spiritual dimensions of their heritage. It is the old way, the way the parents have lived, and they are passing this way on to their children without questioning it. The parents are perpetuating a split in the experience of blessing and property, and the brother and sister identify with opposite sides of the breach. If this old way, which maintains a split between the material and the spiritual aspects of existence, is not healed, the siblings will remain impoverished. Our psychological quest for wholeness suffers from such a split. We can barely survive, but surely not thrive under the conditions it creates. Everyone suffers from this psychic breach, even those very few who end up "living the good life" in outer existence.

The beginning of the tale also gives us more information about the poverty and its roots. (With this new information, and in spite of the fact that this is an ancient Swahili story, this poverty begins to look very familiar to modern-day Western society.) The happiness has indeed been hard won, because the "parents" or dominant conscious mode of being in this family contains a split, which continues after the parents die. As they die, they leave behind a legacy—the continuation of the psychic split. When we feel impoverished, like the "poor" family in the story, there are two possible ways to relate to that feeling. One is to seek riches—that which is lacking—at any cost. The other is to make the best use of what we have. These are the material and spiritual approaches. Ideally, neither attitude need result in a split between the material and spiritual aspects of our lives and ourselves. But in reality they almost always do. And the split occurs in this way: The person who seeks riches becomes consciously split off from his spiritual dimension, maybe even blaming that side of life (the weakness of "emotions," even "God") for the impoverishment he has experienced; meanwhile, the person who makes the most of what he has—"counts his blessings"—embodies the spiritual dimension, but often eschews the material world or is rejected by it. A split between two very basic aspects of life becomes a chronic and pathological condition. Brother and sister cannot thrive in such a split.

So this is the nature of the bond between brother and sister: the brother is identified with the material worldview, the sister with the spiritual one. Neither of them understands that these are two aspects of life—matter and spirit—that belong together, that actually nourish each other. They have inherited this split from their parents, and ironically it binds them to each other. There is a power dynamic in which each is bound to the other as a perpetuator of the negative worldview, the belief that property and blessing can be definitively separated. It is a worldview that doesn't recognize individuation, which necessitates a coming together of the opposites. With this kind of destructive bond, a wound to it could actually look like a good thing. A separation of "brother" and "sister" is always necessary for growth; in this bond it is necessary for survival, at least until some transformation has begun. If brother and sister stay together, they will annihilate each other.

This brother and sister, by choosing one or the other, property or blessing, both believe in and perpetuate the split between these essential dimensions of human life. The sister is as guilty as her brother of living a fragmented life. Who are this sister and brother in our lives? I see this pair everywhere in the modern-day world. He is an exaggerated expression of the "materialistic" world we live in, and she (in the early part of the tale) is a weak but steady energy that keeps reminding us of another—more spiritual—way of living. When someone says that in spite of all the destruction he sees in the world, he still believes in the goodness of the human race, it is the psychic energy of this sister (his sister-anima) that is speaking. However, if not developed, this side of the individual is sentimental and ineffectual as the sister is in the first part of the tale. She loathes herself as she slips off into the forest with her arm bound up, just as we loathe the side of ourselves that, once again can't "make it" in the world (of finance, sport, fashion, whatever the "material" trappings) where it counts. In proper relation, spirit and matter operate together in our lives, each feeding the other, but in a world that values one over the other, the proper relation is difficult to reach.

This way of observing brother and sister is more from a cultural perspective than an individual one. Yet the two are interconnected. In a culture where such a split is often encouraged and lived out, individuals experience the psychological opposites in their most polarized and irreconcilable forms. We have no model for another way, just as the brother and sister of the tale have no model. The "bond" between opposites is negative.

When the sister's hand is cut off, sister and brother have come to an impasse. This particular brother-sister relationship is still in the "bond." They are unable to value each other, and they are unable to separate from each other (the brother expresses this unwillingness to separate by continually "checking" to see if the sister has acquired property). Sister and brother both covet the pumpkins; he sees them as material "property," and therefore belonging to him: she has crossed the line between "blessing and property." There is an inkling of recognition here—the sister senses a connection between the blessing she has received and the property it can produce. The pumpkin vine, a material result of the sister's blessed state, has temporarily taken on the aspect of the Self. But because she too believes in the split, the sister's own form of covetousness takes over— she allows her brother to cut off her hand rather than give him an unripe pumpkin. She has become identified with the little material manifestation of her "blessed" state. That severed hand has grasped the pumpkin vine, an image of the material result of her blessing, and now her one-handedness becomes a symbolic representation of the brother-complex. Both she and her brother are bound to the impoverished view of the world that separates spirit from matter, and neither has faith in his or her own life. They each see the other as the *cause* of their suffering. If ever the alchemical process of psychological transformation were needed, it is now.

into the forest: the first wound

When the sister goes into the forest, it seems to her like utter defeat. Yet, this step removes her from the collective that has bred and perpetuated her subjugation to the brother's demands, that collective ("family") which told her that she must choose between property and blessing. Her relationship to her brother has pitted matter against spirit, and she must learn another way if she can. Here, in the forest, she is mistaken for a spirit by the prince, a mistake appropriate to her development at this point. She is more attuned to spirit than to matter, but she must now attempt to find a new relationship to the world of matter in order to survive. Her missing hand images her near-defeat by the material world.

The prince offers the one-handed girl a union that is safe, and for a time she begins to thrive in her new life. Like the sister-Queen of "Brother and Sister," she needs this time of respite, before she can face the life-changing transformation ahead.

If we think in terms of the sister as a feminine aspect of a young "brother's" psyche, the experience in the forest brings a new development in his masculine identity. He has taken his identification with "property" to its limit, and as his wounded anima retreats, he discovers another dimension within himself. He has nearly lost his split-off feminine spirit, and now he finds himself reaching out to it in a protective and loving gesture. What is that feminine spirit? It may be his artistic life, his love of animals or nature, his feeling of connection to and companionship with others in the world. Or it may be a person in his life who had been undervalued until now. That person could be an actual sister or a carrier of the sister energy, and now the man is beginning to develop an ability to value her and relate to her.

princely love

For the sister, this is a time of separation from the cruel brother-complex, and a time of relationship to a loving masculine presence. It is also a fruitful time: the sister gives birth to a baby boy, an image of her developing relationship to her own creativity. In spite of all the growth that takes place during this phase of the tale, the sister needs to develop further as a woman. There is still a way in which she seems like a disembodied spirit. She is now loved and protected, although we will come to see that the protection offered by her prince is fragile. This sister still needs to learn more about herself and her own transformative feminine nature.

into the forest again: the second wound

Like the girl in "The Handless Maiden,"[4] the one-handed girl must go into the forest twice. In the first experience, she finds the prince. In the second experience, she finds wholeness. This second experience feels much different for her, although her brother has once again forced her into the forest. This time, she goes almost willingly. She has her baby son with her, and we are told that he means more to her than anything else.[5] She is not alone, and the developing potential of the Self is with her. The baby is a much more evolved Self-image than the pumpkin vine from which she was separated before her first trip to the forest. The girl is developing, even though she is still no match for

---

[4] "The Handless Maiden" is another story about a feminine figure whose wounds come from the masculine realm. See "The Handless Maiden" or "The Girl Without Hands" (Brothers Grimm, No. 31, pp. 160-166). The girl's hands are cut off by her father at the request of the Devil. She leaves home, and then later she is sent away from her second home, taking with her the baby boy to whom she has given birth.

[5] See my discussion of the baby in "Brother and Sister," pp. 86-87.

her brother's malice. In fact, part of her development may be that she seems to have learned that neither ignoring him nor fighting him will work. Until this second trip to the forest, the sister has never shown any sign of cunning or trickery. They were the traits of the brother, the one with "property."

The second time in the forest, the sister is again without a plan. She appears to be open to whatever comes her way, and the first thing to come her way is a speaking snake. One of the few "rules" in fairy tales is that it is good to listen when animals speak. The instinctive world has a voice that is often drowned out by our conscious, driven lives. In this case, the sister listens and helps the snake, hiding him in her basket and lying for him. This is her first expression of cunning or trickery. What does this mean? Why help the snake in this way? At first we don't know. However, it is a powerful moment. This young woman has saved the snake from his pursuer, something that she could never do for herself. A new power has awakened in her.

Snakes are very complicated animals, dangerous, even poisonous, yet often helpful and full of possibility. This snake is kind, but he also has the snake attributes of cunning, stealth, and trickery. She has won his trust and his gratitude, and in fairy tale language this means that these qualities (cunning, stealth, and trickery) are now available to her. Very quickly, the snake proves that his is no ordinary gratitude. In a trickster-like maneuver, he restores her missing hand. He makes her "use" that hand as if it were there, and it is instantly restored. His message is that the sister must not live in the confines of her brother-complex. In fact, the snake becomes a "brother" to the young woman, and his is archetypal brother energy. He is her companion and her protector, as she was a protector to him. He takes her to his home to live safely with his parents, and there she connects with the transformative potential within.

So, in her second trip into the forest, the sister stays long enough for her transformation to take hold, and she develops a relationship with the deep power of the unconscious.

the snake world

In this world, the numinous snake family, including the snake-brother, bestows gifts on the sister. First, she is given her hand back; next she is offered seclusion and safety. The brother-snake has connected the sister to the archetypal level of the brother-sister pair, where restoration can occur. Besides, this is a family system where the members are living in a deep harmony and possess riches. The unconscious has compensated the sister's original family experience, in which there was a tenuous harmony lived out in the midst of poverty. A harmonious balance between the worlds of spirit and matter is becoming possible, together with meaning and understanding. The sister dwells in this realm for some time, and it restores her. When she is ready to leave, her baby has grown into a little boy, and she finds herself thinking about her husband. It has taken this long for her to grow into a full woman, or so it seems. Her snake-brother gives her advice as she prepares to leave: he tells her what gifts to ask of his parents, the father's magic ring and the mother's magic casket. Interestingly, they are gifts that will allow for blessing to bestow property, not gifts of property that will soon dry up. She receives magic gifts of "plenty," thus finally joining the worlds that had been split.

the woman returns

When the sister returns from the snake world, she returns as a woman. She has a sense of centered and firm resolve and is no longer dependent on the power of others. She is a woman with a strong connection to the inner experience of the Self which the brother-sister pair can engender. It is her time with her snake-brother and the parent snakes, as well as the ongoing relationship to her child, that has effected this change. She has learned a level of cunning that had been lacking in her previous encounters with her brother and with others. She is able to hide her identity, revealing herself only at the proper time in order to protect herself and her son. She recognizes her brother as the cause of all her misery, and she even recognizes that her growth and transformation would not have happened without him. This is a level of recognition that is rare in fairy tales. The sister is now able to be in the realm of spirit and in the realm of matter, and to bring those two realms together in her life. She has experienced the healing of the split, which had existed for her and her family since before our tale began. Now her husband is able to recognize her. This parallels the recognition at the end of "Brother and Sister"— the husband's recognition of his wife adds validation to her presence. Now the cruel brother is no threat; in fact, he is superfluous and out of place. Thanks to the gifts of the snake-brother, the brother-complex has no power. He is put "out of town."

This story connects us to a deep psychological truth: Blessing and property, the spiritual and the material dimensions of life, cannot be separated without grave psychological consequences. In our world, we are greatly tempted to split these aspects of life, and it is even probable that we *must* go through an experience of this split in order to consciously recognize how much they belong together. This is the Great Work of the alchemists, and the work of our individuation. That a brother and sister act out this separation in the tale is profoundly significant. As the alchemical pair, they are the components of that inner dimension where spirit and matter come together, the dimension of the soul. Where there are brother and sister, no matter how distorted the relationship appears to be, the potential for soul work is present.

2. The Dark Sister: Arthur and Morgause

We all must come to terms with our own darkness, or else suffer its effects throughout our lives, often unknowingly. Darkness comes in many guises. We've seen darkness from outside the brother-sister dyad, as well as within it, in the harsh cruelty of the dark brother. There is also a dark sister, with whom a brother may have to contend. One famous account of her power can be found in Arthurian legend:

*****

In the early days of Arthur's reign as High King of England, it was known that a Northern King, Lot of Lothian and Orkney, was not pleased to submit to the new rule. One day, a woman rode forth to the walls of Caerleon with a small party, and she was Morgause, this rebellious king's queen. Arthur knew nothing of her or of her heritage. Indeed, at this time Arthur did not know who his own mother was. But Morgause knew, and this gave her an advantage.

Among Morgause's party were her four sons—Gawain, Agravain, Gaheris and Gareth. The woman was beautiful and dark, and she requested audience with the High King.

Perhaps there was something in her air that made Sir Kay, Arthur's seneschal and foster brother, suspicious of the Lady Morgause. Some say that, as she passed by him into Arthur's hall, she hissed and whispered, "They say, Ector's son, that your speech was crippled by envy when the High King took your place at your mother's breast." Surely, envy, lust, and greed were strong motivators for this Lady's actions, and she planted their seeds wherever she went.

Before Arthur's throne, she threw herself to her knees and was all feminine softness. She begged forgiveness for her husband's rebellion and asked that Arthur train her sons for knighthood. As Arthur gave her the kiss of peace, she held the king's eyes with her deep green-eyed gaze, and her invitation was clear.

So the High King took Queen Morgause for his mistress, and she and her sons rested at Caerleon for a month. But the pleasure of the bedding had a high cost for Arthur. Some say that a visible change took place for them both. While Morgause grew rosy, Arthur grew ashen as if he were wasting. His sleep was troubled by ominous, haunting dreams. Kay watched all this, but spoke not a word.

By some accounts, Kay secretly sent messengers to search for Merlin. Then, upon his return Merlin interpreted Arthur's dreams, telling him of the enchantress's true relationship to Arthur. He told Arthur that she was his half-sister, and that she now bore a child who was "the sword that will destroy you."

When Arthur went to the tower where Morgause was housed, the room was empty. Neither she nor her boys could be found in the court or on the valley road. It seemed that enchantment speeded and shielded her way.

By other accounts, Morgause left Arthur's court at the end of the month, knowing that she had conceived a child. After she left, Arthur became troubled and uncertain. He dreamed of dragons and serpents. The next day was darkened by the dream; indeed, it was a day more in the realm of dreams than in the realm of the sun.

So Arthur decided to hunt in the forest, and soon he saw a great stag. Most of the day, he gave chase to the stag who was as elusive as a dream figure. His frustration, fears, and the feeling of being inside a dream mounted. It was not for Arthur to fell the stag that day.

Soon, overcome by his dream-state, he rested by a tree, and there he encountered Merlin, who revealed to him his parentage and his folly. In taking Morgause to his bed, he had sealed his own fate. Now she, his half-sister, bore the child who would treacherously bring about Arthur's downfall. She was an enchantress with an eye to the power of rulership.[6]

*****

There are numerous versions of the Arthur-Morgause story. The view of Morgause as enchantress and betrayer is prevalent, although

---

[6] Ellen Phillips, "Morgause," in *The Enchanted World: The Fall of Camelot* (Alexandria, VA: Time Life Books, 1986), pp. 20-35. This version combines elements from Steinbeck, T. H. White, and Sir Thomas Malory. See Bibliography, pp. 203-204.

some versions of the story present her as more neutral, or as a victim of fate as well. I believe that Morgause carries fate in the legends, and as that carrier she is destined to have a sinister quality.

Psychologically, the sister who takes the germ of creation and "disappears" with it has taken on the dark aspect of fate. She has split off from the experience of wholeness that the archetypal brother-sister pair embodies, and her "tampering" (as she sees it) with fate is an attempt to gain power over the brother. Here, the "germ" of creation is the potential child, the only child that Arthur will ever sire. The story creates an image of energy being drained from the young king, and flowing into Morgause, as though she had the seductive power of a vampiress.

In this story, the potential of the brother-sister relationship is distorted and unbalanced. The outcome of such a union can only bring about destructive power, and we know that is exactly what happens in Arthurian legend. The son of Morgause and Arthur grows up to betray and kill Arthur, leading England back to its earlier state of chaos.

What goes wrong in this brother-sister relationship? From the beginning, Morgause knows something of which Arthur is ignorant. Brother and sister are not equal. He believes that this woman is simply offering him a gift, because he is High King. Perhaps this is masculine arrogance, but it is also hopelessly naïve. Arthur remains naïve in the relationship, and the relationship remains unconscious and dangerous because of this imbalance. By some accounts, Arthur senses the destructive powers from the unconscious, but even so he fails to ask the right questions. He is truly representative of masculine energy that has not been mothered. He knows nothing of woman, or how to comprehend her. Had he been nursed and nurtured by his mother's love, he would perhaps be more attuned to the potential danger that this dark woman brings. However, having never known that first and early bond with the feminine giver of life, he is at the mercy of dark feminine energy. It is truly the unknown and the mysterious: he will tend to either over- or under-value the feminine principle, as he does throughout his life.

In brother-sister tales, this poor recognition (or understanding) of feminine danger is frequently the brother's blind spot. The difference is that here the danger comes from the sister, and Morgause uses her brother's weakness against him. The dark aspect of the feminine, which often appears in the guise of a stepmother, mother-in-law, or witch, is *embodied* here in the sister herself. As an embodiment of the negative feminine, Morgause cannot help but give birth to a destructive child. The bond between brother and sister has been "contaminated" by a dark force.

Arthurian legend comes down heavily on this brother-sister union as the "sin" of incest.[7] Many see this heavy-handedness as the obvious Christian influence over an earlier pagan religion, and leave it at that. However, taboos against incest go back much further than Christianity, as do tales of the destructive potential in such a union. The message of taboo here has to do with humans flying too close to the sun, so to speak, or trying to grasp the energy of an archetype. The brother-sister relationship carries the archetypal potential of pure union, but Arthur and Morgause do not move in harmony. As legendary figures, Arthur and Morgause represent a dark aspect of this archetype, an aspect that we would do well to come to terms with.

It is the bond itself, between brother and sister "elements"—that is to say, the bond within us all—that is wounded in the Arthur/ Morgause story. The sister appropriately brings to her brother the potential for relatedness, communion, and soul-making, and she holds the secret knowledge of how relatedness works. Arthur is meeting with his sister-anima, but she keeps relatedness in the dark recesses of the unconscious. Denying "sister" within herself, she crosses over into the lover role.

We can see here that Arthur makes a mistake. He takes the dark woman's "invitation" as his kingly privilege, and he does not ask the right question.[8] Just as the sister of the previous tale grabbed the pumpkin vine and lost her hand, Arthur accepted his "gift" and lost his chance for relationship with his sister.

From that time on, Morgause "appeared to have some secret power over him." Her secret is that they are truly kin. This must mean that Arthur—the shining High King—must, like Morgause,

---

[7] In Chapter 15, the incest theme is handled in quite the opposite fashion, showing us that it is not the theme itself, but the psyche's relation to it, that brings up the destructive forces. See the Selected Annotated Bibliography for further references to incest.

[8] In Arthurian legend, the "right question" is associated with the Grail quest, and is a simple enquiry, "Whom does the Grail serve?" Here, the simple question would be, "Who are you?"

have a dark, brooding, plotting nature, deeply unconscious, which he needs to acknowledge. In Arthurian legend, this side is personified by Morgause, and later by the son she has from her union with Arthur, Mordred.

Sir Kay's watchfulness, and by some accounts his sending for Merlin, is the same kind of watchful energy seen in the huntsmen and the nurse in "Brother and Sister." This attending in the psyche is of utmost importance. However, as is clear in Arthur's story, this watchfulness is not enough to help the King recognize his own shadow and dark anima. Arthur wants to be in the light, he wants to remain identified with the "good king," and that desire could be his downfall.

In the Arthurian cycle, Arthur's coming to terms with his darkness doesn't happen within the brother-sister relationship itself. The stories are many and complicated, and most of Arthur's dark brooding happens within the relationship to his wife and her lover, Guinevere and Lancelot. In order to experience a transformation, Arthur needs to meet a positive sister-figure, as the one-handed girl meets her brother-snake. Instead, his is the story of "one brief shining moment," which becomes engulfed in darkness again.

That shining moment presents such a dazzling image of masculine valor and purity that it continues to captivate the imaginations of young boys and men, perhaps as no other time in our history has. The Arthurian legend of the Grail presents us with an image of the divine sister, in the presence of the Grail maiden, but Arthur's impurity (from this early relationship with his sister) prevents his ever personally encountering the Grail maiden. In a sense, Arthur is more akin to the Grail King, wounded in his ability to regenerate and unable to name his suffering. I can't help but think that it is timely for us to attend to this weakness or flaw in the High King, and to recognize why the brother-sister relationship is at the heart of Arthur's downfall.

When Arthur asks Merlin why he had not warned him of Morgause, Merlin answers that even he cannot foresee everything. Merlin cannot help Arthur overpower the feminine principle any more than he can avoid his own fate, which is to be held captive by a woman who gains his secret knowledge.[9] There is a curse on Arthur's realm,

---

[9] According to legend, Merlin falls in love with a young woman who wishes to gain his powers of sorcery. She traps him in a death-like sleep in a cave, where he "remains to this day."

and perhaps it is the curse of his own beginnings: the deception and rape of Igraine, his mother, by the powerful king Uther Pendragon, his father. This is another part of his life "story" that has been kept from Arthur. It is Arthur's fate to create a kingdom in which women are cherished and protected, only to fall victim to the dark side of the feminine through his vengeful and power-seeking sister.

This sister seeks power through the incest-link. This is in stark contrast to the dark brother in "The One-Handed Girl," who sought power by trying to injure or kill his sister. Morgause instead uses her feminine power to connect, as well as her secret knowledge of kinship, in order to entrap Arthur in a sexual union. He is caught in a regressive relationship to his own sister-anima. Once the entrapment—the incest—has occurred, she can be assured that the dark outcome (their son Mordred) will bring about her brother's destruction. As soon as her deed is accomplished, Morgause leaves Arthur, moving back into the darkness.

When Morgause has left, Arthur has a day of fitful dream-like experiences. One haunting experience during that day is his hunt for the elusive stag. Arthur is both brother and King. The stag should be rightfully his, since that animal is imaginally connected to both the brother and king aspects of the masculine principle. Arthur's failure to fell the stag is a clue that something is not right with his kingly status; his deep spiritual connection to rulership is wounded. Something has gone wrong, has been contaminated, and at its core is the wound to the brother-sister relationship.

The brother-sister connection holds the generative power within the psyche and within the culture. If this connection between the masculine and feminine elements within us is not attended to with loving care and developed internally and externally, both the culture and the individual will crumble.

After he learns the truth of his encounter with Morgause, Arthur attempts to move even more fully into the light, denying his own darkness. Then the darkness itself grows, as Arthur's wife betrays him and his son becomes a man who plots against him. Arthur's story is the story of a brother painfully linked to his sister, yet unable to really know her. There is a rift in the fabric of the psyche, and that rift has wounded the core of the brother-sister relationship. It cannot be healed in Arthur's story. His is a tragedy. All rifts are healable, however, for those who hear the story. And we are the generation of brothers and sisters brought up on Arthurian legend.

CHAPTER THIRTEEN

Bonds That Kill

1. BONDED TO THE GRAVE: "CONSTANTINE AND ARETE"

We Jungians speak of death as representing a major transformation. And it really does. However, when one is going through the experience, it feels like an actual death, like an end, sometimes like a blow. And this is a point in transformation where we can get "stuck" as well.

In long-term relationships, as well as in long-term processes, there is a wide range of variation in the death experience. A kind of death occurs at each transition point. For example, the movement from bonding to wounding is always experienced as a death for the brother and sister. The severity of the wound determines how the "death" is experienced and how the psyche moves into the next stage of development.

Consider these two statements: "My brother and I were always close. His opinions and mine were usually alike. Then he fell in love with a woman I hated!" "My brother, who was the only one in the family that I could talk to, died in a car accident when I was fourteen." I have heard these statements, or slight variations of them, many times. They both express a "death," and shock at such an unexpected end to the brother-sister relationship. Yet both can also be an entrance into the wound that transforms a person's life or tragically marks the end to possibility of actual concrete relationship.

The experience of the untimely death of a sibling can, and often does, bring the psychological development of the grieving brother or sister left behind to a standstill for a while. It is the most severe of all wounds. There are haunting stories about the death of a sibling. One is the story of Constantine and Arete.[1]

*****

"Constantine and Arete"

The Greek traditional ballad tells of a young woman, Arete, who had nine brothers. She married a foreign lover against her mother's will. The mother finally consented to the match, only because Arete's brother Constantine promised to bring her back home if necessary, no matter what the circumstances.

Plague fell on the city. Constantine and all the brothers died. The mother sickened and called for her daughter.

The dead Constantine, true to his word, rode to the foreign country and brought his sister back to their mother's bedside. On the ride, Arete learned that her brother was dead from the birds in the trees as they passed. They commented on the wonder of a dead man riding with a living girl behind.

The girl was brought back as promised. But the mother and sister both died from the terror of the experience.

*****

I have heard so many stories of siblings who lost their brother or sister at an early age. In a number of them, the woman or man speaks of having lived a life, after their sibling has died, as though they were "bonded to the grave." One woman said that after her brother died she lived from her teenage years into her thirties in the shadow of that relationship. This is a dangerous psychological position, and the "shock" that occurs when one realizes he or she is bonded to the grave has a powerful impact. The loss of soul that follows such an experience is inevitable. For some people, years are lost, and then one day an awakening occurs that brings about new life, as in the following story:

There was a young boy who loved his sister very much. She was three years older than he, and she was very beautiful. She understood him, helped him maneuver through their somewhat treacherous family rules, and sometimes she sang him to sleep when he was restless or scared.

_____

[1] "Constantine and Arete," in Funk & Wagnall 's *Standard Dictionary of Folklore, Mythology, and Legend* (New York: Harper & Row, 1972), p. 248.

As the boy grew, his life became more and more complicated. Of course he still loved his sister, and sometimes he would feel a sudden longing for their old bond. On rare occasions, they would sit together and talk. She was still beautiful, and she still understood. She said she was proud of him, and it made him feel better, even during those young teenage years when he often felt confused and ashamed.

The boy was moving quickly now. He was seventeen, a senior in high school, and his life was in high gear. He was a member of the drama club, played guitar, planned to go to college as far away from home as he could. This made him feel guilty when he thought of his sister. She was so delicate and beautiful. She was now twenty, and she was studying at a local college. She lived at home and worked in the school library at night.

Then one day tragedy struck. Driving home from her library job, the boy's sister was hit head-on by a drunk driver. She was killed instantly. The boy thought he would never recover. The rest of his senior year was a blur; even twenty years later, he couldn't remember graduation night. He didn't go to college. He said he felt confused about what he wanted to do. So he traveled. He did odd jobs here and there, and he had some wonderful adventures. Sometimes he felt really full of life, but he always had trouble sleeping. He would get up in the middle of the night and play his guitar.

By his mid-twenties, the young man had more or less settled in the Rocky Mountains. He had also begun to play and sing in little coffee houses and nightclubs. He sang bluesy songs, and he sometimes composed his own.

A frequent theme was lost love, the lost woman, and he often referred to the woman as "an angel." Of course, this was a common enough tendency in song, so the young man had not noticed it particularly.

One night he had the following dream: *He is in a hazy place, and he sees his sister coming toward him. She looks older, like a mature woman, and she says, "My dear brother, you loved me in life and you have searched for me in death. But the angel is not lost."* He awoke with a start.

The young man knew he had been touched by an archetype, and he felt a tremendous sense of release. He spent weeks, then months, pouring out song after song, and this became the content of his first record album. He later would say, "My sister just told me that the 'angel' had to be within me now. And the songs began to spill out, literally."

This young man's sister had been his muse since his early childhood. She sang him to sleep. In childhood, and even at seventeen, we are rarely thinking things like, "What is it in me that this other person seems to represent?" But it is happening, nonetheless. She was his angel, his lost love, and until the dream, he said he felt that his music was "just out of reach." He was bonded to the grave. Now with the sudden new awareness of his "inner sister," this began to change. For the first time in his life, he was becoming consciously connected to his own creative process. And he felt as though he had woken from a long sleep.

2. HOT AND COLD: "THE SNOW-DAUGHTER AND THE FIRE-SON"

Jungian psychology teaches us that the archetype of wholeness and union contains its opposite, fragmentation and disconnection.[2] In keeping with this psychological reality, tragic brother-sister tales and legends in which healing never occurs are found cross-culturally. One such tale is "The Snow-Daughter and the Fire-Son."[3] Here is a brief version:

*****

"The Snow-Daughter and the Fire-Son"

A man and woman, after years of wishing in vain for children, give birth to a healthy and strange daughter, white as snow and cold as ice. They call her simply "our Snow-Daughter."

One day the mother says, "I wish I had given birth to a Fire-Son," and not long after she does. The children are both strong and healthy, but cannot bear to be near each other. When both parents die, the Snow-Daughter devises a plan whereby they can stay together, "going out into the world" in each other's company. She makes fur cloaks for them to wear in each other's presence.

---

[2] Archetypes are considered "bipolar" energies, always containing two extremes (light and dark, negative and positive, etc.). The archetype of wholeness, generally referred to as the Self, likewise has a dark and fragmented side.

[3] Andrew Lang, "The Snow-Daughter and the Fire-Son," in *The Yellow Fairy Book* (New York: Dover Publications, 1966 [1894]) pp. 206-208.

For the first time, they are happy together. In winter, they stayed in a big wood. He built a hut with a fire, she stayed outdoors. The King of the land held a hunt in the wood, saw the beautiful Snow-Daughter and asked her to marry him.

After the wedding, he had a huge underground house of ice made for his wife, and on the outskirts of town he built a house with huge ovens all around it for his brother-in-law. The Fire-Son was pleased, but the perpetual heat made it dangerous for people to be around him.

One day the King invited everyone, including the Fire-Son to a great feast. The guests fled from Fire-Son's heat, and the King said angrily that he should never have taken such a troublesome person into his house. The Fire-Son laughed and embraced the King in a tight embrace, saying, "I love heat and my sister loves cold," and the King burnt to a cinder.

Then the Snow-Daughter ran to her husband, saw he was dead, and, enraged, turned on her brother. They fought fiercely, and when it was over, she had melted into water and he had burnt to a cinder.

* * * * *

This tale is a symbolic picture of brother and sister as extreme opposites. The pair always represents a union of opposites, but here the opposition exists as a dangerous polarization. Just by getting too close, they could kill each other. Even so, when the couple who gave birth to them dies, there is hope of a reconciliation of these opposites. In other words, the collective situation that allowed, indeed "willed," this fierce opposition, fades away. In this transitional time, a new way for the opposites to relate may emerge. It is the sister who is most in touch with the possibilities in the realm of relationship, and she makes the fur coats.

At this point in the tale, there are parallels to the events in "Brother and Sister." The brother-sister pair "goes forth into the world," and they meet a King who is on a hunt in the forest. When the Snow-Daughter and Fire-Son go out into the world, their chance for reconciliation is strongest. They begin appreciating each other. Before this they had only avoided each other. The avoidance is a way of intensifying their opposite natures.

However, the King enters the scene and separates them again, unlike the King in "Brother and Sister," who simply allows the brother-sister relationship to continue. Using his wealth and position, this king creates large structures which keep sister and brother separated, thus again increasing their opposition. In the end, all three die.

The symbolic language suggests a type of consciousness that divides and categorizes its "world," rather than seeking to form relationships within it. It is Logos-directed rather than Eros-directed.[4] Brother and sister, the most "kin" of all relations, are seen as unrelated. The unconscious image of the opposites, the image of fire and ice, is one of such extremes that contact between the two would be sure destruction for both.

The individual's psychic energy is split into seemingly irreconcilable opposites, who are a brother-sister pair. This individual may consciously identify with either the Snow-Daughter or the Fire-Son, thus increasing the sense of polarization.

Some means of bridging the gap between the two is needed, or else the polarization will lead to dangerous inner conflict. Psychologically, the opportunity to bridge the gap arises in the tale when the "brother" and "sister" are no longer consciously connected to the original complex (the drive to overcategorize, represented by the parents). Here again, a brother-sister bond forms when the parental influence is not in the way.

With such an extreme beginning, the pair needs much time in the forest, a physical and mental space free of the influences and pressures of the outside world. There, they may find some way to quell their inner turmoil. An individual carrying these extremes needs to move slowly through his or her internal process before jumping into situations. Hot rage or icy detachment could damage interactions.

The tendency of collective consciousness—our group way of understanding life issues—*is* to separate the opposites. For instance, kids who fight are sent to opposite ends of the classroom. This separation happens between conscious and unconscious as well. For this hot-cold individual, the danger would be extreme one-sidedness: *Either* the Snow-Daughter *or* the Fire-Son could be held in consciousness, accepted by the conscious personality and the greater culture, but never both at once. Such a situation could last for a while, with the risk of contact between consciousness and the dangerous unconscious content growing ever stronger and leading to an inevitable psychological disaster for this individual.

---

[4] Eros is the feminine principle of relatedness, while Logos is the masculine principle that differentiates.

Brother and sister are not in the forest long before the Snow-Daughter charms a King. This unfortunate occurrence ushers the fragile, newly forming personality into the need for conforming, or even relating to the world's expectations far too soon. The fur coat plan just falls by the wayside. It was an ingenious plan, and one that encouraged relatedness between these extreme opposites. Now, the king is the dominant principle in consciousness and in outer life, and his plan is one that separates brother and sister and thrusts them into their own vast spaces. He builds large dwellings for each sibling, thus keeping them more separated than they have ever been. They grow in opposition, and eventually the whole precarious psychic system—brother, sister, and King—is consumed in the heat that this opposition generates in the unconscious. Though they could have been frozen by the sister's ice (and perhaps there exists another story in which they were), here it is the fire-son who has been living on the outskirts of town (in the unconscious) and is therefore the more dangerous to consciousness.

I once worked with a woman in her twenties who had a powerfully negative relationship with her brother. She adamantly claimed that he represented everything she loathed: materialism, chauvinism, "sleaziness," and aggression. This woman prided herself on her life of purity and austerity. She worked hard, ate little, was quite fastidious about diet and exercise, had difficulty with sexual relationships, and was committed to philanthropic endeavors.

When she came to work with me, she was concerned about her tendency to allow men to abuse her. This was not a problem in her marriage, but had been with several other men. She was so polarized in relation to all those attributes she associated with her brother that she had painted herself into a psychological corner. Unless she could begin to broaden her sense of self and learn to live with some of the so-called brother traits—split-off aggression, for example—she would repeatedly attack or be attacked by those traits in the outer world. Since she was identified with the cold Snow-Daughter, the Fire-Son was a real threat in her life.

My work with this young woman focused on recognition of some "masculine" traits within her—her own tendency towards "hot" anger at times, which made her feel guilty; her powerful, even "sleazy" sexual fantasies, which she tended to concretize into the desire for an affair with a dark passionate lover. These were, for her, in the category of "brother energy" because brother was sleazy and she had heretofore always romanticized male-female relationships.

I made a point of not "doing" anything with her recognition of her "masculine traits" when it occurred. Rather, I encouraged her to look at what these experiences might be compensating. She was young and had a long way to go; she needed the protection of the fur coat, which to me meant a simple "being with" instead of "doing with" in the presence of these energies, and she needed a lot of time in the forest.

This woman moved away after we had worked together for a short while. When she left, our analytic work was still in the forest. Perhaps she continued the work on her own or with another analyst. Or perhaps she took off the fur cape and went back to a Snow-Daughter life. Although it had been painful when she came to me, this way of life was not without rewards. The outside world, the world of the King, often pushes opposites apart rather than encouraging integration. The work of the psyche then takes a back seat. As a "Snow-Daughter," my client faced the possibility that her inner work could get "burned up" and she might have to start all over again at some later time, after a considerable amount of emotional pain. This is the legacy of the Snow-Daughter and Fire-Son. There is a grain of hope in their story, but out in the world they are moved to fight each other until nothing is left but cinders and water.

PART FIVE

Incest and Exile

CHAPTER FOURTEEN

Psychological Incest, or the Reluctance to Separate[1]

"THE GLASS COFFIN"

In the lives of brothers and sisters, the experience of bondedness, even when positive, can and does go wrong in a variety of ways. For instance, in prolonged bonding a too-close relationship between the brother and sister is formed, and they avoid relationships with others. When this happens, individuation and the process of connecting to one's own inner strength through the brother-sister dynamic takes yet another twist.

Brother-sister bonding is a powerful experience. Whether the bond is experienced early in life in a familial brother-sister relationship or later in life as an external or internal link with the companion-as-other, it carries a strong pull. The bond may lure the individual into trying to remain in the state of unconscious union or *participation mystique* with the other. This lure can lead to the incest problem which is *inherent* in the brother-sister bond, that of psychological incest. Succumbing to the lure activates an internal trap. The bonding

---

[1] As I state in this chapter, psychological incest is experienced much more often than physical incest in strong brother-sister relationships. It is an experience of closeness that is powerful and compelling, emanating from the brother-sister bond itself, and it can keep the individual from wanting to "grow up" and move out into the world. Even in those relationships where psychological incest has become "experimentally" physical (and mutually tentative), it is typically not experienced as invasive. This is much different from the experience of physical incest in which one sibling is the "perpetrator" (and typically much older) and is more invasive and destructive.

experience which had been healthy and life-enhancing begins to restrict the psyche's growth. Jung's definition of psychological incest is useful in understanding this development:

> Incest is the urge to get back to childhood. For the child, of course, this cannot be called incest; it is only for an adult with a fully developed sexuality that this backward striving becomes incest, because he is no longer a child but possesses a sexuality which cannot be allowed a regressive outlet.[2]

The reluctance to leave the security of the brother-sister bond was apparent in "Brother and Sister" and "The Death of Koshchei the Deathless." However, "The Glass Coffin" is a tale that focuses specifically on this psychological dilemma. The tale begins when redemption is at hand. What has happened earlier in the tale is then related in a flashback:

*****

"The Glass Coffin"

A tailor's apprentice gets lost in a forest, and makes his way to a small hut. A little hoary man lets him in, he spends the night, and is awakened in the morning by a loud noise. A beautiful stag and a great black bull are fighting. The stag defeats and kills the bull, swoops the tailor onto his horns and races away with him. When they come to a wall of rock, the stag puts the tailor down and pushes a door open. A voice tells the tailor to enter, and he walks into a marvelous stone room. The voice directs him to the lower level, where he sees a miniature kingdom in a glass case, and a lovely maiden also in a glass coffin. She opens her eyes, calls him her deliverer, and instructs him how to free her. Upon her release from the coffin, she tells the tailor that she and he will be married that day, and then the maiden tells her tale:

She was the daughter of a rich count. Her parents died when she was young, and her brother brought her up. She and her brother "loved each other so tenderly" and were so alike in their way of thinking, their inclinations, that they resolved never to marry, but to stay together to the end of their lives. There was no lack of company at their castle, they showed great hospitality to their neighbors, and they were happy. But one day a stranger came to the castle and asked to stay the night. They granted his request. The stranger proved very entertaining and pleasant, and the brother invited him to stay on a while.

---

[2] *CW* 5 § 351n.

That night, the maiden was awakened by strange and delightful music, and she found that she could not speak. She was under some spell. Then the stranger, who was a sorcerer, entered her room "by magic arts" and offered her his hand and heart. She rejected him, disliking his magic arts, and he swore to punish her pride.

Before the maiden could reach her brother the next morning, he had ridden forth with the stranger "to the chase." All too late, she found the stranger with a beautiful stag, but her brother was nowhere in sight. When the sister asked for her brother, the stranger laughed. In a rage, the sister then took out a pistol and shot the stranger who was a monster in her eyes.

The bullet merely bounced off him, and it then went into the head of her horse. The sister fell to the ground, unconscious. When she awoke, she was in the cave in the glass coffin, with her castle reduced and enclosed in another glass case. The magician told her that her brother was a stag, and that if she accepted his offer, he would restore everything to her. She would not, and he left her in this very cave.

She fell into a sleep and had many dreams, one of which was of a young man who would set her free, and he was the tailor. So together, she and the tailor released the castle, land, and servants from the spell back to their normal size, as her dreams had instructed. Then her brother walked out of the forest, restored to human form. He had killed the magician in the form of the bull. The maiden and the lucky tailor were married that day.

* * * * *

In this tale, the *participation mystique* or bonding between brother and sister is so satisfying that they both decide never to leave it. This decision, on the external level, is comparable to a decision never to leave home, never to grow up. On the inner level, it is a decision not to accept the challenges of consciousness, of bringing one's thoughts and ideas to fruition, a task that always requires leaving *participation mystique* behind. The two levels go hand-in-hand. A sister and brother may actually live together, choosing never to marry.[3] Or an individual may choose to live a life in which development beyond that childhood state of *participation mystique* never occurs. This is the life of Laura, the stay-at-home sister in *The Glass Menagerie*, whose relationship to her collection of glass figurines is the most real

---

[3] For example, in "Anne of Green Gables," by Lucy Maud Montgomery, the brother and sister (Matthew and Marilla Cuthbert) who adopt Anne have lived this kind of sheltered life. The young, unconventional Anne shakes up their insular world.

relationship she knows.[4] The choice to live this kind of life denies the psyche's flow, resulting in psychological stagnation.

From my own experience and that of a majority of the clients and other brothers and sisters I know, the possibility of spiritual/psychological incest is a danger that may need to be faced at the end of the bonding stage. It is this pleasure in the bond, in the "spiritual union of minds," that is so strong in a brother's sister. This is the picture that the sister in "The Glass Coffin" describes to the tailor. It may be experienced externally in a relationship with one's brother that surpasses any other relationships. *There is so much that she doesn't even have to say*, because he understands her so well.

The strength of this bond can also be experienced internally. The brother's sister tends to have a philosophical bent, and her inner world of fantasy relationships is often experienced as so rich, vivid, and gratifying that the outer world pales in comparison. When that outer world impinges on the harmony she has found, as in "The Glass Coffin," the sister sees it as dark and monstrous. She is romantically caught in a fantasy-experience of the inner harmony of the opposites. There may be a purity and innocence about her, as with Laura, the sister in *The Glass Menagerie*. If, like Laura, she is naturally introverted, the psychological danger of never leaving home is even greater. Her inner life is so alive that she is able to create an imaginal world to keep her safely occupied.

In other fairy tales (and in many life experiences), one of the siblings may resist prolonging the bond. In the Russian fairy tale, "Prince Danila Govorila,"[5] when marriage to her brother is proposed, the sister refuses. She sees this as a sin and struggles to get away from her brother's power. The concept of sin here comes from the collective unconscious, the inner authority that informs us of deep psychological truths. It encourages exogamous over endogamous union.

---

[4] Tennessee Williams, *The Glass Menagerie* (New York: New Directions Publishing, 1999 [1945]).

[5] Previously discussed, pp. 51-52, 76n, 104-105. In this fairy tale, the incest danger appears to be more physical, although in archetypal literature of course we must look at the symbolic level of the imagery, and it has been imposed on the brother and sister by the mother/witch. She offers a magic ring of power to the brother if he marries the woman whom it fits, which is his sister. The incest "curse" is avoided by the sister, who goes on a quest and ends up bringing back another bride—her "alter-ego"—for her brother.

The paradoxical blessing and curse of the brother-sister union is the problem in "Prince Danila Govarila." The explicit threat of brother-sister incest, which takes place when the brother proposes to his sister, is experienced as a wound to the brother-sister union. So brother and sister separate until that threat can be avoided, which happens when the sister finds another bride for her brother. The brother then receives the blessing of his magic ring (promised to him by the witch), when he marries the sister's alter-ego. Sister has brought the right woman to her brother.

This motif of one sibling bringing the right partner to the other occurs in "Brother and Sister" and in "The Glass Coffin" too. In these two tales, the brother brings the marriage partner to the sister. In "Prince Danila Govorila," it is the sister who brings the marriage partner to her brother. In all three tales, prolonged partnership between brother and sister is a psychological threat. However, once a new marriage partner is found, the brother-sister union is freed from being concretely expressed, and can now move toward an inner psychological/spiritual reality.

In the fairy tales, incest is almost always presented negatively, as a threat of death or unconsciousness or, at least, danger. In "Prince Danila Govorila," the brother seeks incest by marrying his sister so that he may have the power of a magic ring. The psyche says this is not the right attitude, that in this psychic structure the brother energy in the woman is temporarily possessed by a destructive power (the negative animus) when he attempts to force the union. Again, in the psychological movement from bonding to wounding, and finally to healing/redemption, the brother and sister must separate. Otherwise neither individual ever leaves the state of *participation mystique*, in which they are merged with one another. "Prince Danila Govorila" shows this merger as a sin against nature. It is a wounding sin against the psyche's goal of individuation. The brother has been lured by the witch and has become one of her voracious beasts, willing, like the wolf discussed in connection with "Brother and Sister" (pp. 49-50), to devour his sister for the magic ring. The incest threat in "Prince Danila Govorila" is different from the incest threat in "The Glass Coffin" because it originates in an outside energy, the witch, rather than from within the of the brother-sister bond itself.

Whether a prolonged bond is sought or desired by both brother and sister, as in "The Glass Coffin," or it isn't, it has a negative consequence. When an individual's development is sacrificed to maintain the brother-sister connection, the image of brother-sister union has become one of psychological bondage, a regressive desire to remain in childhood. The bond itself can lead to this experience, because, like all states of unconscious union, it resists being brought into consciousness. But the transformation of the bond is what psychological development calls for, and it frees the individual's psyche from this regressive tendency.

During the struggle to hold onto the bond, the sister's perception of any masculine energy and the brother's perception of any feminine energy outside the brother-sister bond will be distorted. In "The Glass Coffin," for example, the sister consciously rejects non-brother masculine energy at the beginning of the story, and this rejection eventually causes that masculine energy to constellate as the dark magician.

How the sister responds to this dark magician who has come to visit her and her brother is very telling. First, she enjoys the company of this guest at dinner. He gets her attention. This presents a psychological threat to the brother-sister bond, though the brother and sister are initially oblivious to it. They are unconscious of the psychological split their relationship is creating between them and their own need for development. The brother has even encouraged the man to stay.

In terms of psychological process, let us say that a young woman who has always been close to her brother meets a man who attracts her. The attraction naturally gets the attention of her inner masculine energy (her "brother"). This principle is at work in "Brother and Sister" as well, when the roe-brother wants to join the hunt. Like seeks like, and eventually a woman's animus will want to develop, even at the risk of losing its former shape.

The woman in "The Glass Coffin" *consciously* bolts her door after having made the unconscious invitation, which is her feeling of attraction. Even behind her bolted door, she hears the delightful music of the dark magician and is spellbound. But because of her own dark shadow, which rejects the outside world, she cannot be spellbound without becoming angry, in fact, rageful. She takes pride in her companionable, predictable world, and this new masculine force has invaded it. He has brought up her shadow, which is a murderous madwoman. She sees him as a dark magician and a "monster." Only through her own transformation will she be able to connect to the "good tailor," who is also an aspect of non-brother masculinity.

Marriage, the forming of a new union, is concretely and symbolically a "going forth into the world" to establish a relationship with it. The brother and sister in this story attempt to arrange their lives in such a way as to avoid this process. As a result, the world outside the brother-sister union becomes dark and ominous and shows up on the doorstep of their closed world in the form of an "evil" or "magic" figure.

Often the psychological configuration depicted in "The Glass Coffin" occurs in an actual brother-sister relationship. A former client of mine, after a brief and unsuccessful marriage in her early twenties, moved into a communal home with her brother and some other young people. Since childhood, she had had an idealized relationship with her brother; she saw him as "the way men should be." She and her brother were intellectuals; they were very close and "of like mind." Their ideas about how the communal home should operate were usually the same, and they had a lot of power over decisions in the house because they were intellectually persuasive. Often the other women in the home criticized her because she was so "unfeminine," but the men liked her and told her they "wished more women were like her."

Life in the communal home, where she and her brother reigned as intellectual monarchs, was a concrete manifestation of this woman's psychological development at the time. Her brother-animus was idealized; she knew how to be a sister, an equal intellectual companion to men, and this was her chosen way of relating to the world. This "chosen way" was the way of reason, and, she necessarily conducted her relationships reasonably. She denied the emotional failures of her love relationships, and secured herself within the brother-sister bond.

Like the maiden in "The Glass Coffin," this woman had blocked out the potential emotional messiness of relationships with men who were not so perfectly aligned with her as her brother was. Such relationships were a risk because they would usher her into a new stage of psychological development. In that stage, she would be clumsy and unsure of herself, a state she dreaded.

After moving from the communal home, she had the following dream:

My brother and I are in a tall building with a black man and some other people. The black man keeps taking people out of the room, and when they return they are different.

My brother and I realize that they have become evil and that the black man is an emissary from Satan. He intends to take over the world, and we must fight him. My brother and I escape and begin to gather together the good people who are left. Often, we run into the Satan people and have to fight them. At the end of the dream, I am inside a cave with a small group of the good people. The Satan people are coming from the other end with torches. It will be the showdown. A farmer-type man is saying to us that we have been missing what we must have in order to win the battle. He looks over our heads, and as I turn to follow his gaze I see a "vision" of Jesus, beautiful and standing in a ray of light.

The dream's farmer is a figure similar to the tailor in "The Glass Coffin." Both are masculine figures who can be trusted, and they serve as mediator between the powerful archetypal energies and the woman's ego; thus they are positive male figures who are not so caught up in the struggle.

In the young woman's dream, the farmer introduces the transformational figure of Jesus. The power of this transformational figure is undeniable, although it felt mysterious and undecipherable to the dreamer at the time. In the fairy tale, the tailor is also able to assist in the transformation of the sister's enchantment through very simple acts—opening the lid of the coffin, listening to her story, opening the glass jars to release her enchanted kingdom.

The dreamer had been attempting to fight Satan, the dark side of the Self, with her inflated brother-sister bond. That bond is merely the first stage in the transformation of brother-sister energy, and it cannot replace the Self. The brother's sister must struggle with her negative complexes to realize the brother-sister union (Self). She had wanted to avoid these struggles, the "messiness" of new kinds of relationships *and* her own insecurities about them. Her "vision" of Jesus encourages the struggle at an even deeper level than this woman had imagined; symbolically, he represents the spiritual and transformational level of the Self. She awoke from the dream *knowing* that it had presented her with a spiritual challenge to develop her life beyond the intellectual world she had made for herself.

Sometimes dreams give us information or show us connections that we don't recognize, and such was the case in this woman's dream. There is a set of medieval alchemical plates (three of which are shown in Fig. 1) that depict the transformation of Sol and Luna (sun brother and moon sister, as can be seen in Plate 2), who personify the opposites. The final plate in the series (Plate 20) represents the transformed couple (shown coming together in Plate 13) as an image of the Risen Christ.[6] Thus, the woman's dream echoes a solution laid out by alchemists as early as the sixteenth century: the transforming of the two, Sol and Luna, into the holy one, Christ, an androgynous and transcendent figure. This dream and its associations give a new and satisfying meaning to the often-heard phrase, "Jesus our brother."

In her outer life, this intellectual brother's sister unwittingly became more susceptible to her own negative animus (the brother's unconscious or shadow side). By the time she "fell into" a relationship, it was with a brutal and unreasonable man, who was an outer embodiment of her negative animus. Now in her mid-thirties, this woman is free of that relationship and is piecing together

---

[6] See Lionel Corbett, *The Religious Function of the Psyche* (London: Routledge, 1996).

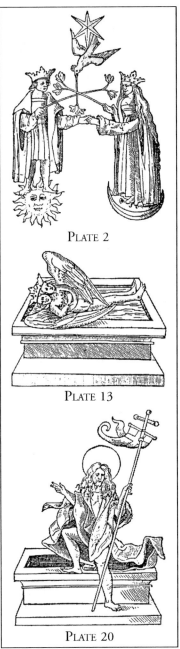

PLATE 2

PLATE 13

PLATE 20

Fig. 1: Three plates from the series *Rosarium Philosophorum*

a new way of relating to herself and to the world. With the energy of the tailor, she is sewing together the fabric of her life.

When positive brother-sister bonding is prolonged, vulnerability and susceptibility to more negative masculine or feminine energy develop. For example, the sister in "Brother and Sister" marries a good king, and her resistance to his entry is relatively brief. Instead, her difficult struggles are with a dark mother figure. In "The Death of Koshchei the Deathless," Prince Ivan struggles mainly with the dark masculine power of Koshchei, and also has to eventually encounter Baba Yaga. A battle with some dark and unconscious force is necessary for the individual to become strong and perhaps diversified enough to go back and reclaim the brother-sister energy as his or her own rightful possession.

In outer life, at first, the siblings may tend to experience other neglected archetypal forces that they encounter as one-sided, and these forces often attack them from the unconscious through enchantment (or "theft," as is Koshchei's maneuver[7]). These attacks can come from the negative mother, the negative animus or masculine energy, and/ or the dark father. Each attack ultimately has the potential to increase the strength and endurance of the brother-sister pair. For example, the sister who has struggled with her negative mother-complex is capable of giving and receiving nurturance while maintaining a sense of her own authority and equality with others; a brother who has faced his own brutal shadow is able to combine masculine strength and even spiritual power with a sensitive and companionable nature; and the sibling who has come to terms with the destructive side of the father can model harmonious relationships while battling the injustices in our world.

Prolonging the bond with the brother or sister is a regressive, even incestuous, process that weakens the ego as well as the potential of the inner experience of the brother-sister pair, rendering the sibling more susceptible to attack from those negative forces. In other words, to prolong the bond leads to the very thing that it attempts to avoid. We can't help but grow up. The companions must battle with the negative forces and experience the transformation of this powerful

---

[7] In "The Death of Koshchei the Deathless," Koshchei steals Prince Ivan's wife, Marya Morevna, and this leads Ivan to his most profound challenge and his greatest transformation.

inner bond into its creative (*coniunctio*) potential. The relationship of brother and sister actually *has infinitely more* potential than the bonded sibling can imagine. Only by letting go, and moving into new regions of his or her life's journey, can he or she hope to connect with all this potential.

CHAPTER FIFTEEN

Forbidden Union

In his work on the incest taboo in primitive cultures, John Layard relates a very intriguing and unusual myth about a culture-hero named E-rets. This myth was told among the people of the Atchin village near the Malekulan mainland where he had lived at one time.[1] The story goes like this:

*****

"E-rets and Le-rets"

E-rets had a sister Le-rets, who married and moved across the river from her family's village, as was the custom. Perhaps E-rets had always loved her, but when she was to move his love grew stronger. He took her aside and told her privately that, "If a cock crows overhead in the sky," she should leave her home and secretly come to meet him. Then he built a kite of "mythic proportions" which held a cock, and flew it across the lake over to her home. Le-rets saw and heard the cock, so she stealthily went to meet him. They stayed in hiding together in his hut, but of course they were fated to be found out. When they were found, their family and the villagers alike drove them from the village. On their way, a stranger came up to E-rets and offered to help them to be accepted by the villagers.

*****

After the village accepts E-rets and Le-rets, further myths about this pair inform us that the village doubles in number and size. Accepting the brother-sister pair has benefited the community and increased its scope.

---

[1] John Layard, "On Psychic Consciousness," in *The Virgin Archetype* (Zurich: Spring Publications, 1972 [1959]), pp. 328-333.

But exactly what is the heroic action that is taken in this story? Layard explains that E-rets's actions, in defying custom and marrying his sister, represent a social revolution that was then taking place in this culture. (Myths are the form of archetypal literature that is most linked to cultural influence, so a discussion of cultural patterns in relation to this particular story is in order.) Rather than representing actual incest (or psychological, we should add), a crime for which a couple would have been killed in this culture, E-rets represents a man "so closely allied to his sister-anima that he could challenge the world, and at the same time improve it, and be approved by it."[2] That is to say, E-rets was a man who acknowledged his internal, sister-feminine nature. It is significant that the anima in this story is sister, because brother and sister *are* the best possible figures to represent the pair of opposites who *can* "change the world, improve it, and be approved by it." This quote speaks to the creative work of the questing spirit, the Self energy that emanates from the brother-sister pair.

Interpreting a myth of this nature is a difficult and delicate process. Like the gods and Egyptian Pharaohs, E-rets is a figure who has performed an act—marrying his sister, or incest—that is not sanctioned by the collective. Yet this story says that at a deeper level, if we embrace the union that his action brings about, we will be blessed (as seen in the story in the expansion of the village). Why is incest "right" in this tale, when it is "wrong" in "Prince Danila Govorila" and many other tales? In fairy tales and myths, an act that is right in one story may lead to utter disaster in another. We must look at the specific psychological experience that is presented in each story.

This tale is not actually condoning or elevating either psychological or physical incest in the outer world of personal relationships. Rather, it is speaking to a deep psychological wound that has stricken the very heart of the brother-sister union. The Atchin village knew that wound, and so do we. When recognized, it must be healed. Perhaps, as with the fisher king's wound in the Grail legend, it is the recognition of the wound that brings about healing. What is this wound?

---

[2] Layard, p. 333. In fact, it is very important not to confuse Layard's interpretation with a sanctioning of psychological or physical incest. The psyche's experience of psychological incest is an intra-psychic pattern (mirrored by inter-psychic relationships) of libido cycling back on itself or "regressing." Layard, on the other hand, is speaking of the intra-psychic experience of discovering one's own contrasexual nature, thus transforming that regressive pattern.

Some cultures wound the psyche, the very psyche that they originally were organized to protect, for protection of the individual psyche is one psychological "reason" for the formation of cultures. These cultures have often succumbed to the lure of linear progress, an approach to life that denies the value of relatedness or "eros."[3] In such a culture, there is very little harmony or working together, either on the inner level for the individuals of that culture or for the people as a whole. The culture becomes a "dog-eat-dog world," and the majority of the individuals within the culture feel driven by the rules or status quo rather than experiencing their own power to change the rules. Apparently, the Atchin village was one such culture, for the tale of E-rets and Le-rets is a tale of a psyche so split and wounded that it had to defy the whole cultural environment (laws, ethics, living arrangements) in order to be whole again.

The culture that can wound the psyche is no stranger to us, since we live in one. There are men's groups and there are women's groups, and yet communication across the gender line leaves much to be desired. Divorce rates continue to rise, and abuse is flagrant. We are not in harmony, as most of us are painfully aware. Our culture encourages "individualism" at the expense of the individual and competition at the expense of relationship.

This disharmony is found not only in the external world, but in our internal life as well. How can we expect to embrace diversity among cultures when we deny the shadow within ourselves, projecting it onto individuals and whole cultures that are radically different from ours? Men and women who can't get along with each other also suffer from inner turmoil. Whenever women and men reject each other, they are rejecting their own inner masculine and feminine natures, animus and anima, not recognizing their own potential for wholeness.

The "brother" dimension of the psyche is a good space in which a woman *and* man may begin learning about this potential for wholeness. "He" is an aspect of masculine energy that is not ruled by the patriarchy. The story of E-rets is about brother energy asserting itself in the face of masculine order and authority. It is also a story of love.

What can the story mean, if taken to be a girl's story, or the story of a girl's development? Psychologically, the girl who is being married off to a man not from her village has been taken further and further away from her brother-nature. Layard tells us that the Atchin village enforced this strict marriage requirement. The girl does not live in a world where the companionable aspect of masculine nature is valued, but rather this world uproots her and forces her to fit into the rules of exogamous union. Yet a part of her still lives far "across the water," a symbolic statement that means she is bound to an unconscious place where brother-sister (endogamous) union still exists. In speaking of endogamous and exogamous tendencies, Jung says that, "the two forms together hold each other in check."³ A culture whose wounds can be healed by the psychological and symbolic experience of brother-sister marriage is a culture in which kinship libido has been lost to the onward progression of logos. A restoration of balance between the two ways of being—exogamy and endogamy or logos and eros—is the goal of this symbolic "marriage."

It is the individual's inner life, in the image of brother-sister union, that is given a chance to live again in "E-rets and Le-rets." Perhaps if a culture has split itself off from concern for the individual's inner life to an extreme extent, such a myth must come along to compensate that situation.

The culture-hero speaks for the inner life, and in this story he does this very directly. E-rets must assert the power of the "original bond" personified by brother and sister. The regeneration of culture is his goal.

The heroic action of E-rets (literally "he who speaks") is to speak in support of the union of opposites, symbolized by his union with his sister, and to defy the very structure of his village's social system which requires a strict separation of the brother-sister pair. He breaks the law, and he does this by marrying his sister, an act that is abhorred by the people. He chooses to live in the union which, "above all else depicts a human encounter where love plays the decisive part."⁴ One must expect to be unappreciated and misunderstood when one begins the quest for such an inner experience. And yet, paradoxically, if one can actually pull this off, holding the tension of opposites internally (in the brother-sister union) and externally (between the individual path and societal expectations), it will surely result in blessing. This is a hard road to travel.

---

³ *CW* 16 § 431.
⁴ *CW* 16 § 419.

Nine times out of ten, the societal structure seems to shatter the inner life of the individual. Society, to preserve itself, must be impenetrable; it cannot allow too much deviation among the individuals in its ranks. And yet if an individual can stand up to the collective (society) and assert that his or her own relationship to life is the right one for him because it honors a union in love, suddenly the whole psychic picture alters. A figure appears, like the stranger in this myth, who "shows the way" for the unconscious content—the experience of brother-sister union—to connect with the world. This figure is a kind of psychopomp,[5] and, as such, knows the value of the hero's statement.

Layard has uncovered a myth that challenges the very fiber of our collective existence, and such a myth must be approached with care. Like the alchemical image of brother-sister marriage, it is likely to be misunderstood and cast aside as "rubbish" or looked upon with horror and disgust. It speaks of the *prima materia*[6] from which gold is extracted.

E-rets makes a simple declaration of love, and it is a love of his own inner world, his anima. This act makes for a very unique kind of hero. He honors "the human encounters where love plays the decisive part," and the family and villagers finally allow E-rets to come back. Redemption is found in a humble act of love.

The culture-hero is the conscious manifestation of what we hold in high esteem, as good, enduring, larger-than-life. He or she is an image of the Self. Yet the culture-hero whose life is a representation of this brother-sister union must follow a twisted path leading to the place of exaltation. This is not a hero who goes out and does great deeds, bringing treasure and glory back to the kingdom. It is a hero who shows the collective that which it most abhors: that the inner world of the individual is more enduring than the outward structure and laws of the society. This is a challenge, for it asserts that the laws must speak for the individual or they are doomed to fail.

---

[5] A symbolic figure who personifies the teacher aspect of the Self, the "one who shows the way."

[6] In alchemy, the primordial substance, often literally refuse or decaying matter, which is rejected by the collective and by the ego, but contains the potential for new psychological understanding.

In that inner world the brother-sister pair "stands allegorically for the whole conception of opposites."[7] This pair unites the opposites in a simple relationship of companionship and love. This is a rare and powerful relationship for the opposites to share, and it creates a rare kind of Self-image: the hero who breaks the culture's strongest taboo by loving his inner feminine nature. This is the brother's challenge.

---

[7] *CW* 12 § 436.

CHAPTER SIXTEEN

The Exiled Brother: Three Bird Tales

The exiled brother brings us face to face with the possibility of the "brother" and "sister" potentials in the psyche being "lost" to each other before either has had an opportunity to connect with or even know of that potential. In "Brother and Sister," as in the other tales I have discussed earlier, where the bond is positive, sister and brother already have a strong bond before they are separated. However, in the exiled brother tales, the sister and brother are denied access to each other through a forced separation often before a bond has formed between them. This indicates that there is a pre-existing psychological one-sidedness that resists the emerging brother-sister pair before that potential even takes shape. The exiled brother tales present a resistance that separates brother and sister, showing a particular hostility to the brother, but does not (as does the witch in "Brother and Sister") attempt to destroy both siblings. The girl-child is spared, and in fact coveted in some of these tales. This one-sidedness that resists the pair has put into place conditions that, for a time, rule over the new potential in the psyche.

In fairy tales, often it is the father who exiles the brother. The father perhaps may have been starved for positive feminine energy, and so when a daughter is born, he wants to possess her, forgetting or growing hostile toward his sons. The psyche is out of balance. Father is unable to let the young girl grow and interrelate with her "brothers." He is threatened by the potential brother-sister union, as was the evil stepmother in "Brother and Sister," because it may deprive him of something that *he* needs, like the young feminine energy of his new daughter.

There are three strikingly similar brother-sister fairy tales about the motif of the exiled brother, all from *Grimm's*: "The Twelve Brothers,"[1] "The Seven Ravens,"[2] and "The Six Swans."[3] In these tales, the fates of brother and sister are interwoven, yet there is a strong archetypal energy that pulls them apart early in the story, before they have had time to become conscious of their connection. And, the brothers in all three stories are enchanted into bird-form.[4]

In "The Twelve Brothers," a daughter is born to a couple with twelve sons. The father wishes to kill his sons so that all his wealth will go to his daughter. However, the mother warns her sons of the father's intention, and they leave home and live in the forest together. They swear an oath that they will kill the first maiden they see, because of the injustice done them by the birth of their sister.

Meanwhile, after about ten years, the sister learns of her brothers' existence from her mother, and she goes into the forest to seek them out. When she finds them, the youngest brother persuades the others to forsake the oath they have made to each other to kill the first maiden that they see (their sister) so that the sister and her brothers can all live together for a while. Then, by "accident," the sister brings about the enchantment of her brothers. She picks flowers which have magical power over the brothers; these flowers turn them into ravens, and they fly away.

An old woman tells the sister that to return her brothers to human form she must neither speak nor laugh for seven years. During this time, she marries a King whose evil mother tries to prove that she is a witch. On the final day of her seven-year silence, she is to be burned as a witch because of the accusations made against her by her mother-in-law. The brothers appear at the last moment, become human again, and rescue her. Only then is she able to tell her story to save herself. The King's evil mother is killed, and the brothers, sister, and king all live happily.

---

[1] Brothers Grimm, No. 9, pp. 59-64.

[2] *Ibid.*, No. 25, pp. 137-139.

[3] *Ibid.*, No. 49, pp. 232-237.

[4] As I stated earlier, birds and brother energy have a psychological connection. This was the form taken by the sisters' husbands, who themselves were powerful shape-shifters, in "The Death of Koshchei the Deathless," as well as the form taken by my brother and me in my childhood dream, related on pp. 27-28.

In "The Seven Ravens," a daughter is born to parents who have seven sons. Again, the father has wished for a daughter. At her baptism, the father becomes angry with the sons when they are not prompt in fetching the baptismal water for their sister, and he unthinkingly says he wishes they would turn to ravens. The brothers do turn into ravens and fly away. Years later, when the girl learns of them, she goes to set them free of their curse. After various trials, the sister finds her brother-ravens, they become human, and sister and brothers return home together.

"The Six Swans" fairy tale presents the motif of the exiled brother from a somewhat different angle. A good but somewhat weak father marries an evil sorceress against his will (he is tricked into the marriage by the mother of the sorceress). He already has seven children—six boys and a girl—and he hides them from his wife. The sorceress finds the boys and turns them into swans, but she can't find the girl. When the father learns what has happened, he wants his daughter to stay at home with him, but she insists on leaving to search for her brothers. As in "The Twelve Brothers," the only way the sister can redeem her brothers is by remaining mute for many years. She also must sew shirts of starwort for them during this time.

As she is fulfilling these tasks, a king falls in love with her, they marry, and she has three children. At the birth of each child, the King's evil mother sneaks the new-born away, accusing the sister of having killed it. When the sister is about to be burned as a witch (for killing her children), the brothers appear. The sister throws the shirts she has made on them, and they are all returned to human form—all but one wing of the youngest brother. The sister is saved and reunited with her husband, her three children, and six brothers.

In the first two tales, the sister doesn't know for several years that she has brothers. The father has been unable to maintain a connection to his sons while welcoming his new daughter into the world. Representing the dominant masculine principle, he tends to romanticize his daughter and to favor her over her brothers: he gives her all his riches (in "The Twelve Brothers"), or places importance on her baptism over the lives of his sons (in "The Seven Ravens"). She is idealized, but only as a one-dimensional sweet caricature of femininity, the "girl-child." Unlike her brothers, who could potentially replace the father, she is no threat to the father's supreme authority. The father can love her without fearing that she will usurp his power.

The father in these tales seeks power over his offspring, as does the stepmother in "Brother and Sister." This desire for power is most evident in "The Twelve Brothers" and "The Seven Ravens," but even in "The Six Swans" there is a hint of it in the fact that the father wants the sister to stay with him once her brothers have been enchanted. This desire for power is two-fold. First, it is an expression of competition in the masculine realm between father and son. (Just as the stepmother competed with the sister for feminine power in "Brother and Sister.") The father can actually covet the sister (his daughter) as long as she is the "only child" but rejects and even seeks to destroy— in "The Twelve Brothers"—the brothers (his sons).

The other aspect of this rejection or desire for power relates directly to the brother-sister relationship itself. Interestingly, in "The Twelve Brothers" and "The Seven Ravens," the father does not reject his sons until the daughter is born. This indicates that the father also fears or is resistant to the brother-sister pair, not just the brothers who may compete with him for power. Initially, the father principle in these tales prevents brother and sister from getting together, thereby delaying the formation of the brother-sister bond.

It is imperative, then, if the daughter is to remain this sweet feminine caricature, that she not connect with her brothers. As we have seen in other tales, and as this father senses, the sister aspect of feminine energy is no sweet caricature of femininity but is instead characterized by the questing spirit. When a female connects with brothers, and consequently with the brother side of her psyche, she begins to develop a strength of character that does not serve this power-driven "father." If he is to maintain control, he must prevent that development.

The father as King represents the masculine principle in its highest form of development within the culture or the collective consciousness (the culture's collectively recognized values, opinions, and beliefs). His attitude in these tales suggests that there is a tendency to overvalue the feminine principle as it is embodied in the daughter as a prize (as in "The Twelve Brothers" and "The Seven Ravens"), or undervalue it as a witch (as in "The Six Swans"). The father rejects the sons, favoring his daughter, but he does not know how to "bring her up." He covets her as a novelty and separates her from the rest of his "creations."

Sometimes an actual father (or the masculine authority) keeps brother and sister apart and prevents them from knowing each other. In my experience, most cases of extreme sibling rivalry have this dynamic at the core. The rivalry springs from an overemphasis on the parent-child relationship (father *or* mother) coupled with a de-emphasis or even severe limitation of the sibling bond. In an actual family situation, the siblings may be subtly or blatantly encouraged to compete with each other for the parents' attention rather than to relate to each other as companions; they are prevented by the parents from forming a bond with each other.

The most extreme example of this psychological dynamic of parental control of the siblings' relationships with each other, coupled with the father's covetous attitude toward his daughter, is father-daughter incest. This is a pathological system in which the girl-child is kept "Daddy's little girl" at the cost of developing her own individual life independent of her parents. My first experience as a therapist was working with adolescent prostitutes. Many of the young girls I worked with had been their fathers' incest victims. They didn't know how to relate to men in any way other than through sexuality, but they had a fierce longing to learn. In my work with these girls, we read myths and fairy tales, and I was interested to find that they gravitated toward the stories in which chaste females were either solitary (like the Greek goddess Hestia, for example) or were strong sisters sharing power with their brothers. They themselves were "sisters" who had been coveted by the father, and thereby kept away from their exiled "brother" energy. The path to healing and to reconnecting with this brother energy for such a young woman is steep and difficult.

The father in the exiled brother fairy tales secretly fears the way of being that is personified in brother-sister union, and he seeks to prevent its emergence. Psychologically, his resistance to the brother-sister union is an unconscious acknowledgment of its power in the psyche. This father is also a fragment of an original brother-sister pair, now cut off from his "other half"[5] and therefore from his creative potential, and he is driven by a one-sided urge for power. His wife is either weak or dead, and has been replaced by a witch.

To keep two opposite ways of being—masculine and feminine—in focus at the same time is exceedingly difficult. The negative mother

---

[5] See "The Family Archetypes in Conflict," pp. 41-45.

and negative father archetypes are more commonly observed in our psychic processes and the collective environment than is the image of brother-sister union or the *coniunctio*. That union is difficult to achieve and meets with many obstacles. There is a strong tendency to reject the brother-sister pair, and that tendency is in control early in the "exiled brother" tales.

However, the brother-sister bond symbolizes another powerful psychological reality, the archetype of the union of masculine and feminine—the "hostile opposites"—in a harmonious, companionable relationship. This archetype has a strong pull all its own. So, at the end of the ten years, in "The Twelve Brothers," something new begins to happen, moving the girl-child out of her limited role as the sweet caricature of femininity. The sister learns that she has brothers, and at a time in life when young heroes and heroines often set out on their quests, she begins a quest to find her brothers. In effect, she is searching for the potential brother-sister union, which is her birthright.

At this point, the image of the brother-sister bond has begun to emerge in the sister's psyche. The brothers are an inner reality that resonates with the sister as soon as she learns from her mother that she has brothers in the external world. Finding her brothers is her first solitary individual task; it sets her apart from her father's world. She is on the road to individuation and the transformation of the brother-sister bond.

In "The Six Swans," the brother-sister bonding is more interrupted than delayed. Otherwise the story is very similar to "The Twelve Brothers." The father is a weak masculine figure who marries a witch against his wishes, and she fills him with "secret horror." Then he attempts to hide his children from her. When the brothers are enchanted by the witch, the father seeks to keep his daughter with him, but she goes in search of her brothers. The brother-sister bond was interrupted by the father's weakness, or more specifically by the lack of brother-sister union between the parental figures. (As I have stated elsewhere, mythology and alchemy point us to this powerful psychological reality: The original "parents" in our psyches may very well be the brother-sister pair.[6]) The young brother-sister bond is then "sacrificed" by the parents, so the siblings themselves (especially the sister) must take up the task of re-establishing the bond.

---

[6] See p. 42.

In the case of the "exiled brother," bonding between "brother" and "sister" occurs at a different point in psychological development than in many of the other stories I have discussed in earlier chapters. In "Brother and Sister," for example, the bonding stage takes place early in life and is comparable to an experience of *participation mystique*. In the "exiled brother" stories, no bond has formed early in life between brother and sister (or the bond has been severed before it is fully developed), so that the sister's urge to bond, to be united with her "brothers," comes later in life, at a time when the "sister" may well have already struggled with the energies of the mother and father complexes. Initially, she will still experience the bond as a *participation mystique*, but her worldly awareness and ego development will perhaps render this bonding stage less hazardous than it is in "Brother and Sister." Many women I know—clients, friends, and family—do not connect to brother-sister energy until they are in their thirties or forties.

Likewise, a brother who is exiled has already been in the woods ten years before he connects to his sister, as in the stories "The Twelve Brothers" and "The Seven Ravens." Obviously, his masculine development has had more of an opportunity to take shape and is more intact by the time he meets his sister-anima than that of the young man who grows up with a sister. As is often the case, the development that would have taken much longer at a younger age moves more quickly for the older adult who is discovering the brother or sister energy for the first time.

In the exiled brother tales, these developmental differences are imaged in various ways. There is a feminine maturity in the sister's ability to go through her introverted (silent) phase of the bonding stage without the physical presence of the brothers. For example, in both "The Twelve Brothers" and "The Six Swans," at a time when she is longing to be with her brothers, the sister must endure a number of years of silence. These two more mature sisters even marry during this period without the brother's "prodding" or the signs of resistance that were present in "Brother and Sister." Also, the brothers in all three tales have a life all their own for some time away from their sister. They live in a cabin or live as birds together, and they know each other well before they join with the sister. Masculine identity is further developed, and can help the exiled brothers to connect to their sister when she re-enters their lives.

I had a client who did not begin to recognize until she was in her thirties that her long-standing antipathy for her brother was cultivated by her parents, who cast her as the "good child" who would follow their expectations and her brother as the "problem child." The parents had delayed the formation of a bond between her and her brother, but could not hold her back from following her path. In her thirties, she began to remember and have dreams of a potential deep union with her brother. Her positive brother-animus was coming out of exile, inviting her to enter into a new kind of relationship with the unconscious, imaged in the brother-sister pair.

In the 1960s, a generation of brothers and sisters found each other. They called themselves various names, "hippies" being the most common. As a member of that generation, I can recall the fierce loyalty we professed to each other's individuality and equality. After what we felt was a repressive pigeon-holing and stereotyping of males and females by our parents' generation, we were the generation who wanted to find liberation. We called one another "sister" and "brother" by way of recognition. Whatever impact the young generation of that decade had on human history, it stands as a psychological image of the exiled brother and sister finding each other at last.

PART SIX

The Questing Spirit

CHAPTER SEVENTEEN

A Sister's Voice: The Questing Spirit in "Mr. Fox"

T he dynamic combination of brother and sister may potentially form what I call the "questing spirit"[1] in a woman (or man). Quite simply, this is an experience of creative and harmonious energy directed toward truth-telling or uncovering an important psychological reality—the heroic action of going into the unknown or even dangerous place and bringing a truth to light. It is a potential in *anyone* who begins to connect with the brother-sister archetype. The experience of the questing spirit has a pull all its own, which is related to the great pull that brother-sister energy exerts on an individual. In its nascence the questing spirit may have puer-like features. It can manifest in a somewhat foolhardy or reckless tendency on the part of the sister to take on dangerous situations. In the English fairy tale "Mr. Fox,"[2] the brother's sister is challenged by the horrors of a dark and murderous force, and her questing spirit emerges in full focus. The story goes like this:

*****

"Mr. Fox"

A young woman named Mary lived with her four brothers in a village in the wild isolated land of the moors. Mary was the most beautiful young woman in the village, and she had been wooed by many of the young men of the village. She rejected them all. They were just village boys, and

[1] See p. 41n.
[2] "Mr. Fox" in *Chillers,* record album, Connie Regan & Barbara Freeman, Mama-T Artists, 1983.

she envisioned for herself a different life than any of them could offer. A handsome stranger named Mr. Fox, whom some called Reynadine, came visiting in the village, and he chose to court Mary. He was different from the village boys, and she loved to hear him tell of far-off places. One of her brothers was always present when he called. Little was known of him, but he told Mary that he lived in the wood north of town. She was surprised and said that no one ever went to that wood because it was evil. Mr. Fox just laughed at this silly notion, saying that someday he would take her there.

One day while picking wildflowers, Mary wandered into the wood, got lost and saw a house. She thought it might be Mr. Fox's house, and she became curious. A sign over the door said, "Be bold, be bold." She went in and wandered up the stairway to a door that she thought would be Mr. Fox's bedroom. A sign over that door said, "Be bold, be bold, but not too bold." Then she went in and looked around, opening a closet door. Over that door a sign said, "Be bold, be bold, but not too bold, lest that your heart's blood should run cold." In the closet were tubs filled with bones, blood, and human hair of women.

Frightened, Mary turned and ran out of the room and down the stairs. Then she saw through the window that Mr. Fox was coming, pulling a woman who was resisting and screaming. Mary hid under the stairway. He came in with the woman, and when they were on the stairway she swooned. Mr. Fox tried to pull a gold ring off her hand, and when he couldn't get it off, he pulled out a knife and cut off the woman's hand. The hand fell in Mary's lap. Mr. Fox couldn't see the hand, so he dragged the woman up the stairs and into his room, where he shut the door. Mary kept the hand in her pocket, ran out the door and straight home.

When Mr. Fox next came to court, Mary made sure all four brothers were with her. Mr. Fox asked why she was so quiet, and she said she had dreamed a strange dream. He implored her to tell it, and she told all who were there, as though it were a dream, the story of her recent adventure into the wood:

"I dreamed that I went to your castle, Mr. Fox, and it was in the woods, and over the door was written: 'Be bold, be bold.'"

Mr. Fox said, "But it is not so, nor it was not so!"

Mary said, "But that is how it was in my dream, Mr. Fox."

And she went on, "And when I came to the door to your room, over it were the words: 'Be bold, be bold, but not too bold.'"

Then Mr. Fox said, "But it is not so, nor it was not so!"

Mary again said, "But that is how it was in my dream, Mr. Fox." And she went on, "When I was in your room, a closet door caught my eye, and over it were the words: 'Be bold, be bold, but not too bold, lest that your heart's blood should run cold.' And I opened the door, and that room was filled with blood and hair and bones of poor dead women."

Mr. Fox was growing quite agitated, and he said, "But it is not so, nor it was not so!"

Mary said, "But that is how it was in my dream, Mr. Fox. And then I ran out of the room and down the stairs. Just as I was by the door, I saw you, Mr. Fox, coming across the lawn, dragging a poor lady, rich and beautiful."

Mr. Fox said, "It is not so, nor it was not so. And God forbid it should be so."

Again Mary said, "But that is how it was in my dream, Mr. Fox. And then I hid myself beneath the stairs, and as you came in dragging the lady up the stairs, you tried to pull a ring off her finger. Then you took out a knife and cut her hand right off."

Mr. Fox stood up and said, "But it is not so, nor it was not so, and God forbid it should be so!"

Then Mary said, "But it is so, and it was so. And here's the very hand to show." She took the lady's hand from her dress and put it on Mr. Fox's plate.

Mary's brothers immediately seized Mr. Fox, took him out back and killed him.

*****

This is a powerful and chilling tale. Who is Mary, the young woman who seeks out Mr. Fox's true nature and is courageous enough to bring that dangerous nature to light? First we are told that she lives with four brothers. Their parents are nowhere in the tale. The brothers appear to protect her—one is always on hand when Mr. Fox visits. Mary is curious about the world around her. She wants to move out into it; this is implied at the beginning of the story in the statement that she had rejected her local suitors, but accepted the stranger who told her of "far off places." Her desire to explore takes her into the woods, where at first she wanders unconsciously and where she has been told Mr. Fox lives. So, from the first Mary is a sister with a keen interest in the world around her, who feels comfortable exploring that world, *perhaps* because she knows that her brothers are ready to protect her. At first, her self-confidence and curiosity may seem merely naïve, as though the "faith in her own life" that the brother-sister bond has given her has made her "too bold." In fact, a brother's sister often appears on the surface to have a foolhardy belief that she can handle what comes her way, and she will sometimes be carried into dangerous realms.

Mary has a restlessness (seen in her discontent with the local boys), a curiosity, and a belief in herself, all of which come together once she enters the forest. These attributes then form a guiding force, which is the questing spirit that directs her on her journey. She proves to be more than merely foolhardy; she is a well-developed brother's sister who can go into the source of danger and find her way out again. Her questing spirit is absolutely essential to bring the "truth" she discovers in the forest of the unconscious back to the light of day, to consciousness. A mature brother's sister like Mary possesses the courage to act. Symbolically, this is the roebuck brother's energy, discussed in the "Brother and Sister" fairy tale, internalized. The theme of a young woman revealing the murderous nature of a man and bringing him to justice is paralleled in other tales, such as "Blue Beard"[3] and "Fitcher's Bird,"[4] but in none of them is the heroine quite as bold as in "Mr. Fox." In "Mr. Fox," the sister, through her boldness, finally exposes the murderous fiend to her brothers, who know exactly how to dispose of him.

In psychological language, this tale images the process in which a feminine ego explores to its very core the evil in the collective shadow and negative animus realms, encounters it carefully, and has the animus strength and sense of timing to bring that evil to judgment. During the process, Mary must recognize her own shadow, personified in the swooning woman whose murder she witnesses. Mary has a strong will, and her shadow is helpless femininity, the victim. However, when the woman/victim's hand falls in Mary's lap, Mary is hiding under the stairs—a moment of truth for her. In hiding, she has curbed the potentially foolhardy side of her questing spirit, which could have led her to confront Mr. Fox without the back-up of her brothers, and she has accepted that more passive side of femininity that can hold an experience without acting on it. She wins her own struggle with the collective shadow and negative animus when she takes the dead woman's hand, thus accepting (befriending) her own shadow nature.

---

[3] Lang, pp. 290-295. In fact, the motif of the murderous man with a secret room where he keeps the remains of his victims is often referred to as a "Bluebeard" motif. In both "Blue Beard" and "Fitcher's Bird," the maiden's brothers play a role, but that role is shared by sisters and other kinsmen in "Fitcher's Bird."

[4] Brothers Grimm, No. 46, pp. 216-220.

The proud, sometimes even pompous, nature of the brother's sister, which rejects many "feminine ways," has to be let go of in order to accomplish this simple task of accepting her more passive shadow. Her tendency to see herself as set apart from other women and not having anything in common with them goes by the wayside next to the tubs of hair, blood, and bones, and the murdered victim's hand. In addition, the brother's sister personified in Mary has to put in perspective any former feelings of being the special one chosen by the mysterious Mr. Fox. Her specialness is in her ability to expose him, not attract him.

The sister's story at the end of "Mr. Fox," told as though it were a dream, holds everyone spellbound, including Mr. Fox. This motif of the sister telling her story appears over and over in the brother-sister fairy tales. We have seen it, for example, in "The Twelve Brothers," "The Six Swans," "The One-Handed Girl," and "The Glass Coffin." For a woman, the questing spirit is, in one sense, simply the power of a sister's voice. As a woman develops an awareness of her inner experience of the brother-sister pair, her questing spirit develops as well. It generates in her a spirited desire for truth and the active energy necessary to bring to light the truth of the dark unrevealed side of life. Her voice is the culmination of all the struggles that have brought the sister full-circle in her transformation process. With the energy of the Self, and the faith given her by her brother-sister union, she speaks the truth that she has brought back from the depths of the unconscious. And her voice rings as clear as a bell.

CHAPTER EIGHTEEN

A Brother's Love: The Questing Knight's Return in "The Laidly Worm of Spindelston Heugh"

Perhaps the "going forth" aspect of the questing spirit is less unusual in a young man, so the brother who possesses this quality does not seem as unique a character as the sister who possesses it. But the questing spirit of a brother is not like that of most other young knights on the hero's journey—it is characterized by love. It is this depth of feeling that goes into his quest that sets him apart from other courageous young men. For example, Prince Ivan in "The Death of Koshchei the Deathless," discussed in Chapters 8-11, illustrates the love and depth of feeling that characterizes the brother's questing spirit. These feelings appear when Prince Ivan has to weep and weep whenever he loses, or thinks he has lost, his wife.

The English fairy tale, "The Laidly Worm of Spindleston Heugh,"[1] is a tale in which a questing brother's love saves his sister:

*****

"The Laidly Worm of Spindleston Heugh"

In Bamborough Castle lived a king who had a fair wife and two children. The son was named Childe Wynd, and the daughter was Margaret. Childe Wynd went forth to seek his fortune, and not long after this the queen died.

The king mourned, but one day he saw a lady of great beauty while hunting, and he decided to marry her.

---

[1] Jacobs, pp. 183-187.

Princess Margaret handed the keys to the castle to her stepmother, when she arrived. But one of the knights exclaimed at Margaret's beauty, and this made the new queen angry.

The queen was a witch, and that night she turned Margaret into a "laidly worm" or dragon. The spell could not be broken until Childe Wynd returned and kissed the laidly worm three times. The dragon slithered away.

The laidly worm reached the Heugh or rock of the Spindlestone, and there she lay. The people of the countryside learned to control the laidly worm by giving her milk to appease her terrible hunger. A mighty warlock told them also that the loathsome thing was really the Princess Margaret, and only Childe Wynd could restore her to her natural shape.

When Child Wynd heard the news, he swore an oath to rescue his sister. He took thirty-three men, they built a ship and made its keel of the rowan tree. Then they set sail for Bamborough Keep.

When the ship came near, the stepmother summoned imps to keep the ship from landing. But they had no power over the rowan tree. So she sent the laidly worm, and made it fight the ship.

Whenever Childe Wynd came close to the shore, the loathsome thing fought him back with its horrible tail. He did not know this dragon to be his sister, and the witch's power forced the sister to fight Childe Wynd away. Three times she fought the ship off the shore.

Finally, Childe Wynd turned the ship away from shore, and the queen thought he had given up. But he really rounded the next point and landed safe. He rushed on shore to fight the terrible Worm that had kept him from landing. But once he had landed, the witch-queen's power over the laidly worm was gone, and the witch went back to her bower alone.

When Childe Wynd came rushing up to the dragon, it made no attempt to stop or hurt him, but when he raised his sword it spoke in his sister's voice:

"Oh, quit your sword, unbend your bow, and give me kisses three. If I'm not won ere set of sun, won never shall I be."

Childe Wynd wondered at this, but finally he kissed the loathsome thing once, twice, and three times, and the Lady Margaret returned to her natural shape. He wrapped her in his cape, and when they returned to the castle keep, he touched the witch-queen with the twig of the rowan tree, and she turned into a huge ugly toad.

It is said that at times, to this day, a loathsome toad can be seen haunting the neighborhood of Bamborough Keep.

*****

At the beginning of this tale, Childe Wynd the brother goes forth, leaving sister and parents. He is a "brave youth" who rides forth like the wind, and just as thoughtlessly. His sister is safe at home when he leaves, but shortly after he departs all this changes. Childe Wynd has not properly attended to his sister-anima, and she becomes dragonlike (chaotic, rageful, unpredictable) when he leaves her to her own devices.

The masculine hero's journey is under way, but with a different twist, since the story is really all about the sister who is left behind. Once the brother leaves, the sister is attacked by the witch-mother. She is a common threat to sisters in the brother-sister tales, as we have seen in earlier chapters.

How might this psychological situation appear for a man in his outer life? With a sister-anima that has become a dragon, he would be a dreadful and unpredictable companion. In true dragon-form, he would have moody outbursts and a devouring nature, which must be handled carefully lest they get out of control (just as the villagers had to control the laidly worm). Woe to the man who attempts to leave his anima out of his life because "she" will rise up from time to time and destroy his rational, orderly life.

In "Brother and Sister," the siblings worked out a balance between the tendency to go out into the world, always personified in the brother, and the tendency to stay in, always personified in the sister. However, in the story of Childe Wynd and Lady Margaret the need for balance goes unheeded when Childe Wynd goes away. His departure leaves his sister vulnerable, and communication between them does not occur for some time. Naturally, the result is devastating.

Eventually, across the waters of the unconscious, Childe Wynd hears the message that things are not well "at home." It is the brother-sister relationship that calls him back, and fortunately for the psyche, he heeds the call.

According to this story (and many others), the fates of brother and sister are intertwined. The warlock says that Childe Wynd must return to Lady Margaret in order to make right what has gone wrong in his kingdom. When Childe Wynd left his sister, his departure created an early wound to their bond. In order for that wound to be healed, brother and sister must be reunited.

But reunion is not all that must occur. Childe Wynd must first overcome his own tendency toward masculine aggression, seen in his initial impulse to rush to slay the dragon that kept him from landing. Previously, when he left home, he rushed off thoughtlessly, and his sister was unprotected. This time, the result of his impulsivity could be even more devastating. He must stop and listen.

As Childe Wynd listens, again a sister's voice speaks the truth that underlies external appearances—as she, still in dragon form, tells him that he must kiss her three times in order that she may "be won." Now, the brother must not only hold his sword of aggression, but also kiss the loathsome dragon. He must embrace what his sister has become in his absence.

To recognize or accept one's dark side is difficult. It is a testimony to "brotherly love" and also to the balance that the brother-sister archetype can bring that Childe Wynd is able to stop his fighting and to kiss the dragon three times. Now brother and sister are united, and together they can deal with the witch-mother and put the kingdom back in order.

The brother's task is to hear his sister's voice and to allow feeling and love to be a part of his questing energy. Without these three components—sister's voice, love, and feeling—questing is reduced to masculine aggression. The questing spirit of the brother-sister archetype is a balance of masculine and feminine, going forth and coming home with the voice of truth.

Redeeming Brother and Sister in Our Lives

The brother-sister relationship has collective as well as individual significance. Certainly the struggle for equality is a part of our cultural heritage. It is ongoing and we are not alone in that struggle. Equality, as well as liberty and justice, are terms we use often and experience seldom. We rarely have relationships that are not hierarchical in nature.

The brother-sister relationship, however, is about equality and companionship, not competition. It is not just about the family of origin, but also the family of humankind. The competition between brother and sister, commonly called "sibling rivalry," is not so much an inherent aspect of their relationship, but is something that happens when siblings must vie for parental and other adult attention. Sibling rivalry may be a part of one's development, but it also frequently hides the potential that exists in the brother-sister connection itself. Perhaps that potential seems an ideal, but it is not an unattainable one. We must begin by seeing that it—like the Self (in fact, it is an aspect of the Self)—is within each of us.

To turn one's analytic gaze toward the internal energy of the brother-sister pair is to begin an active and hopeful process that will ultimately bring us closer to one another as brothers and sisters.

To my mind, there is a profound need for those in the analytic profession to understand both the nature and the transformative potential of the archetypal brother-sister pair because inevitably this archetype will manifest in the psychic structure of an individual during the course of an in-depth analysis. Typically in analysis, brothers and sisters as dream images are taken fairly literally; that is, they are interpreted on the personal level with the dream brother or sister figure representing the actual brother or sister of the analysand in the external world. This is, of course, an appropriate beginning, but it is also a reductive approach, which cannot on its own connect the individual with the brother-sister archetype. Even when analysts work with the relationship archetypally, they frequently assume that brother and sister are merely aspects of the father or mother archetypes. This is a fallacy. A great disservice is done to the human potential for relatedness when the brother-sister archetype is not analyzed in its own right.

As I have shown, the image of the brother-sister pair underlies our human existence. It is an image of union between opposites, and the union is characterized by love, mutuality, and equality; these characteristics are contained in an experience of companionship.

The image itself inspires strong reactions which seem inconsistent with one another. One reason for this is that when brother-sister union becomes the central archetype in an individual's development, it draws the envy and hostility of other split-off archetypal forces in the unconscious, namely the dark sides of the mother and father archetypes. Often the symptoms arising from a clash between the inner brother-sister pair and one of these archetypal forces will be mistaken for a pathology inherent in the union itself. So pathology gets projected onto brother and sister.

Out in the world, polarization is much more the norm than is the balanced harmony represented by the brother-sister pair. We tend to live in extremes, identified with one or the other "side." Yet, if the message of this pair—a message of equal and harmonious relationship—is not heard, we may all end up cinders and water.

Another reason why the image of brother-sister union inspires strong reactions is that it brings us in touch with a central paradox in the human condition. The brother-sister pair represents a blessing and curse for the individual and for us. The pair may be collectively exalted, or it may be looked upon with disgust. Both responses can occur simultaneously. The individual for whom brother-sister union is a central archetype must meet and struggle with the paradox. Ultimately, this is our collective struggle, for the brother-sister image is important in our culture now.

What exactly is the paradox of the brother-sister pair in human terms (as opposed to archetypal terms)? On one hand, the brother-sister pair may represent a tendency toward psychological incest or regression that keeps either sibling from moving out into the world. But, on the other hand, it may also represent a tendency toward psychological transformation. In psychological language, incest and transformation are opposites, and all the brother-sister tales seem to point to this: the bond between brother and sister becomes either a place of stagnation or leads to a transformation of the highest order. The brother-sister archetype, and specifically the union of the brother-sister pair, represents each of these human experiences.

In the fairy tales, sometimes the sister and brother "live happily together all their lives," sometimes they separate tragically, sometimes theirs is a relationship of struggle and heartache. This is how the inner dynamic works in our lives. The brother-sister relationship provides a multifaceted image of the potential within us all. It is a potential for loving companionship, for breaking bread together, and for going into the world with a fierce desire for truth and equality. Within this potential, there endures a loyalty to the life generated by devotion to its inner source.

The tales take the sister and brother within us through the painful and rewarding journey of their own life's development. That journey begins with the powerful bonding of equals. This is followed by the wounding that the relationship suffers as we each struggle with our own growing up. There is a further wounding that is suffered in feminine and masculine identity. Our culture denies the potential complexity of both genders, and we are all wounded by this denial. As brothers and sisters, we suffer together equally. We can reach our own salvation and ability to restore each other to a new level of humanity if we attend to the brother-sister pair within. The tales give us hope, for over and over again the brother-sister pair has gone into the wide world, and in its suffering has created a psychological space in which the life of the individual can thrive.

Selected Annotated Bibliography

Bank, Stephen P. and Kahn, Michael D. *The Sibling Bond.* New York: Basic Books, 1982.

Bank and Kahn have made an impressive contribution to the understanding of siblings generally and how important they are to one another. As therapists, they interviewed over 250 cases. Over and over, their research reflected the power of the sibling connection. While Bank and Kahn did not focus specifically on the brother-sister relationship (except in a section on brother-sister incest), their observations are, nevertheless, useful in understanding it. One of their emphases in the book is on revealing siblings "in their own right," not merely as parental substitutes or extensions. Bank and Kahn recognize ways in which siblings are different from parents, and they conclude that "the life-long quest for a secure personal identity is inextricably woven into that of one's sibling" (p. 111). This attitude allows a differentiation between sibling and parental relationships. For example, one of Bank and Kahn's findings is that sibling bonds become stronger when the parents have been less available or have been negative influences in the family structure (p. 111).

Cicirelli, Victor G. *Sibling Relationships Across the Life Span.* New York: Plenum Press, 1995.

Victor Cicirelli sees a shift in psychological research, which is beginning to take into account the importance of sibling relationships. Previous thinking, he states, was that the parents were primary influences on behavior and development in childhood and adolescence, and peers were the primary influence in adulthood and old age. He attributes the new interest in sibling influences partially to the emergence of family systems theory (p. 1). Three of his descriptions of the unique qualities of siblings are of interest to this study: (1) that they have the longest relationship over a lifetime; (2) that their relationship is characterized by a "relative egalitarianism"; and (3) that they have a long history of shared as well as non-shared experiences (p. 2). Further, Cicirelli speaks of the impact siblings have on each other's development in terms of its relative independence from parental influence. He states, "Researchers have begun to realize that siblings have a major impact on one another's behavior and development through mutual socialization, helping behaviors, cooperative tasks and activities, and simple companionship, as well as through aggressive and various other negative behaviors" (p. 6).

Kawai, Hayao. *The Japanese Psyche: Major Motifs in the Fairytales of Japan.* **Dallas, Texas: Spring Publications, 1988.**

Hayao Kawai refers to brother-sister fairy tales in Japanese folklore. He speaks of the brother-sister relationship as having a strong effect on his culture and points to fairy tales and the significance of the relationships between brother and sister in those tales. Kawai speaks of the spiritual powers sisters hold in Japan specifically, but he also refers to several Grimms' tales, saying that the spiritual power of sisters can work either positively or negatively (p. 74). One of the ways in which the spiritual power can be experienced as negative is when the bonds between sister and brother are too strong, and the development of the psyche is fixed at that stage. He refers to the tale "White Bird Sister," saying that this tale really refers to a stage of sister-brother union, not to marriage. This is similar to Jung's idea that the brother-sister relationship is an expression of endogamous libido.

Jung, C. G. "The Psychology of the Transference." *The Collected Works of C. G. Jung.* **Eds. G. Adler, M. Fordham, W. McGuire, & H. Read. Trans. R. F. C. Hull. Vol. 16. Princeton, NJ: Princeton University Press, 1946, § 353-539.**

In his work on the transference, Jung cites "Prince Danila Govorila," a Russian brother-sister fairy tale. In contrast to his work with the alchemical concept of the pair, Jung looks at brother-sister incest in that tale in terms of anima and animus dynamics. He refers to endogamous or "kinship libido" and its opposite, the exogamous form, which he sees operating in the tale. The first makes the brother tend towards marriage to his sister, an "evil fate that cannot easily be avoided" (§ 431). The second form makes him tend towards taking a stranger for a marriage partner. The tale clearly moves with the purpose of sparing the sister from incest with her brother. This purpose is accomplished when the sister finds her "alter-ego" (§ 430), whom the brother marries.

The contrast between the Russian tale's treatment of brother-sister incest and the alchemical brother-sister marriage brings up an implicit paradox in the archetypal relationship of brother and sister: at times the brother-sister bond is seen as a marriage of the highest order (as with alchemy or the Egyptian Pharaohs), and at times it is seen as a horrendous and unpardonable sin or crime against nature and humanity (incest taboo). In his writing, Jung addresses this paradox: he sees the paradox related not so much to concrete incest as to the idea that such a powerful combination as the incest union, "whether of brother and sister or of mother and son, ... symbolizes union with one's own being" (§ 419). The inner experience of this union—individuation, becoming a self—always presents human nature with a paradox. As individuals and as a culture, we struggle to find the balance between inner development and outer advancement. This paradox is addressed in the pages of this book, as well as the peril inherent in the individuation quest itself.

Kerényi, Carl. *Zeus and Hera: Archetypal Image of Father, Husband and Wife*. Princeton: Princeton University Press, 1975.

In this work, Kerényi deals with the mythological theme of brother-and-sister marriage. He sees this marriage as symbolic of a "pre-human state," or archetypal realm, in which the gods engage in activities not intended for humans. As an archetypal experience, the "pre-human state" is like the alchemical vessel in which brother-sister union ("*hieros gamos*" or sacred marriage) brings about a mystical transformation.

There are two important messages in Kerényi's emphasis on this "pre-human state." One is that on the actual human and interactive level, brother-sister sexual union is not seen as a spiritually transformative experience. It "threatens the propagation of the human race," putting the siblings in danger of the "reabsorption into the motionless unity of the primordial condition" (p. 113). This is the danger of being fixed in the primitive state of "*participation mystique*," or unconscious identity with the object. Kerényi is saying that if incest is "acted out" on a physical level, both brother and sister could fail to grow up or develop psychologically beyond that state of primitive identity. They would then be caught in the concrete union.

Another message in Kerényi's emphasis on the pre-human state of Hera and Zeus has to do with the mythological theme of which their union is a part: brother and sister as "the mythological origin and beginning of everything" (p. 96). Symbolically, this union must therefore contain a wealth of creative potential and energy. Kerényi's focus is on archetypal patterns represented by Zeus and Hera, one of which depicts brother-sister union as the very basic element from which human consciousness is born.

Layard, John. *The Virgin Archetype: Two Essays*. Zurich, Switzerland: Spring Publications, 1972.

Layard addresses the brother-sister relationship in terms of incest and its taboo. He sees the incest taboo as representing an inner truth—contrary to a popular view that it is strictly an external, social law—and states, "the ultimate authority in the taboo is the collective unconscious" (p. 263). In other words, Layard is suggesting that in the collective unconscious, there is a "right way" for brother and sister to relate, and that the incest taboo is connected to that "right way." To paraphrase Layard, the incest taboo is a message to consciousness from the collective unconscious, to strictly forbid endogamous union. It is easy to see that cultures can get stuck at the concrete level of the taboo, however that is only the beginning of the psyche's "mandate," according to Layard.

Layard further states that the outer taboo is an indication that this forbidden union "can and must be satisfied in the spirit" (p. 265). This is the incest paradox. On the one hand, the taboo comes from an inner authority; on the other hand, the concrete union it forbids is a spiritual necessity. This contradiction is intrinsically linked to the mystery of the brother-sister relationship, and Layard sensed this mystery. On a spiritual level, he saw brother-sister union as man's need to develop awareness of the sister within. Layard is speaking of the intrapsychic experience of discovering one's own contrasexual nature, thus transforming the regressive pattern of libido cycling back on itself (psychological incest).

Mitchell, Juliet. *Mad Men and Medusas: Reclaiming Hysteria*. New York: Basic Books, 2000.

Juliet Mitchell's study of hysteria explores the influence of the "lateral relationships" of siblings, peers, and affines (marital partners). She points out that siblings present us with our first "social" relationship, and they are "the great omission in psychoanalytic observation and theory" (pp. 20-23). Mitchell boldly states that once we think of siblings, "[they] come out of their hiding places and are everywhere noticeable" (p. 24). She brings the sibling relationship into the forefront of the psychoanalytic study of hysteria.

Sanders, Valerie. *The Brother-Sister Culture in Nineteenth-Century Literature: from Austen to Woolf.* New York: Palgrave, 2002.

Valerie Sanders has studied famous brother-sister pairs as well as literary/ philosophical references to that relationship during the nineteenth century. This is a rich study, affording many literary and psychological (though not stated as such) insights. Sanders writes of the relationship as an ideal and safe companionship, in which "men could be trusted to behave, and women were allowed to show their feelings"(p. 4). She makes an interesting connection between the power of that relationship and the British Royal family in 1841— the year when Victoria and Albert gave birth to their second child, "Bertie," thus sealing the public's image of the balanced royal family: father and mother, brother and sister. Even though Victoria gave birth to nine children in all, "there remained something significant about the first two as a brother and sister pair" (p. 11). This makes me curious about my own generation, the "hippie generation" to which I alluded earlier (p. 180), and the possible influence of our beloved "first family:" Jack and Jackie and their children, John and Caroline.

Schmidt, Lynda. "The Brother-Sister Relationship in Marriage." *Journal of Analytical Psychology* **25 (1975): 17-35.**

Lynda Schmidt takes up the task of combining brother-sister and husband-wife to arrive at what she considers a useful model of archetypal patterns for modern-day marriage. The brother-sister pair she uses for that model is Apollo and Artemis (sun and moon). In her references to Apollo and Artemis, she speaks of two aspects of the brother-sister relationship: a kind of overall equality and equal authority. With Apollo and Artemis, the equality is related to their origins—they are twins, and as children they were always together, so that whatever one experienced the other experienced. Later, as sun and moon, they rule equally, each over his and her own domain (day and night). Thus, they both exercise authority within their harmonious existence.

It is Schmidt's contention that the brother-sister aspect in male-female relationships allows for equality, with neither member in a position of authority over the other. She works toward a model in which brother-sister energy can be part, though not all, of the relationship between husband and wife.

Throughout her paper, Schmidt focuses on relationships between men and women, with only brief references to the inner journeys these relationships may reflect. Her goal, I believe, is to validate marriage as "an arena for the struggle between a woman and a man" (p. 17). She posits that "[f]or those who began in childhood in an alliance with the opposite sex parent (positive or negative), or with a strong sibling relationship (positive or negative)," a relationship model of brother-sister/husband-wife might work better than the traditional husband-wife model (p. 32).

Bibliography

PRIMARY SOURCES

Benny and Joon. Dir. Jeremiah S. Chechik. 1993.

Blake, William. *The Portable Blake.* New York: Viking Press, 1968 [1946].

"Blue Beard." In *The Blue Fairy Book.* Comp. Andrew Lang. New York: Dover Publications, 1965 [1889], pp. 290-295.

"Brother and Sister." In *The Complete Grimm's Fairy Tales.* Comp. The Brothers Grimm. London: Routledge & Kegan Paul, 1975, pp. 67-73.

"Constantine and Arete." In *Funk & Wagnalls Standard Dictionary of Folklore, Mythology, and Legend.* Ed. Maria Leach & Jerome Fried. New York: Harper & Row, 1972, p. 248.

"Fitcher's Bird." In *The Complete Grimm's Fairy Tales.* Comp. The Brothers Grimm. London: Routledge & Kegan Paul, 1975, pp. 216-220.

"Hansel and Gretel." In *The Complete Grimm's Fairy Tales.* Comp. The Brothers Grimm. London: Routledge & Kegan Paul, 1975, pp. 86-94.

"Juan and Maria." In *Filipino Popular Tales.* Ed. Dean S. Fansler. Hatboro, PA: Folklore Associates, Inc., 1965 [1921], pp. 295-301.

Kawai, Hayao. "White Bird Sister." In *The Japanese Psyche: Major Motifs in the Fairytales of Japan.* Dallas, TX: Spring Publications, 1988, pp. 207-212.

Malory, Sir Thomas. *Le Morte D'Arthur.* New York: Modern Library, 1994.

Montgomery, Lucy Maud. *Anne of Green Gables.* Toronto: Bantam Books, 1978 [1908].

"Morgause." In *The Enchanted World: The Fall of Camelot.* Alexandria, VA: Time Life Books, 1986, pp. 20-35.

"Mr. Fox." *Chillers.* Record album. Connie Regan and Barbara Freeman. Mama-T Artists. 1983.

"Prince Danila Govorila." In *Russian Fairy Tales.* Comp. Aleksandr Afanas'ev. Trans. Norbert Guterman. New York: Pantheon Books, 1973 [1945], pp. 351-356.

Riding in Cars With Boys. Dir. Penny Marshall. 2001.

Shephard, Sam. *Fool for Love.* San Francisco, CA: City Light Books, 1983.

Steinbeck, John. *The Acts of King Arthur and His Noble Knights.* New York: Farrar, Straus and Giroux, 1976 [1952].

Tennessee Williams. *The Glass Menagerie*. New York: New Directions Publishing, 1999 [1945].

"The Death of Koshchei the Deathless." In *The Red Fairy Book*. Comp. Andrew Lang. New York: Dover Publications, 1965 [1890], pp. 42-53.

"The Girl Without Hands." In *The Complete Grimm's Fairy Tales*. Comp. The Brothers Grimm. London: Routledge & Kegan Paul, 1975, pp. 160-166.

"The Glass Coffin." In *The Complete Grimm's Fairy Tales*. Comp. The Brothers Grimm. London: Routledge & Kegan Paul, 1975, pp. 672-678.

"The Laidly Worm of Spindleston Heugh." In *English Fairy Tales*. Comp. and ed. Joseph Jacobs. New York: Dover Publications, 1967 [1898], pp. 183-187.

"The One-Handed Girl." In *The Lilac Fairy Book*. Ed. Andrew Lang. New York: Dover Publications, 1968 [1910], pp. 185-208.

"The Seven Ravens." In *The Complete Grimm's Fairy Tales*. Comp. The Brothers Grimm. London: Routledge & Kegan Paul, 1975, pp. 137-139.

"The Six Swans." In *The Complete Grimm's Fairy Tales*. Comp. The Brothers Grimm. London: Routledge & Kegan Paul, 1975, pp. 232-237.

"The Sleeping Beauty in the Wood." In *The Blue Fairy Book*. Comp. Andrew Lang New York: Dover Publications, 1965 [1889], pp. 54-63.

"The Snow-Daughter and the Fire-Son." In *The Yellow Fairy Book*. Comp. Andrew Lang. New York: Dover Publications, 1966 [1894], pp. 206-208.

"The Three Ravens." In *The Oxford Book of English Verse, 1250-1900*. Ed. Arthur Quiller-Couch. Oxford: Clarendon Press, 1919, p. 360.

"The Twelve Brothers." In *The Complete Grimm's Fairy Tales*. Comp. The Brothers Grimm. London: Routledge & Kegan Paul, 1975, pp. 59-64.

White, T. H. *The Once and Future King*. New York: Berkley Publishing Corporation, 1958.

Yeats, W. B. "Crazy Jane Talks With the Bishop." In *The Collected Poems of W. B. Yeats*. New York: MacMillan Publishing Company, 1950 [1933], pp. 254-255.

SECONDARY SOURCES

American Heritage Dictionary of the English Language. Ed. William Morris. New York: American Heritage and Houghton Mifflin Company, 1973.

Clark, Brian. "The Brother-Sister Marriage: Opposite Sex Siblings and Their Impact on Adult Relationships." Astro*Synthesis, Applied Astrology for Human Development. 1999. <www.astrosynthesis.com.au.>

Corbett, Lionel. *The Religious Function of the Psyche*. London: Routledge, 1996.

de Vries, Ad. *Dictionary of Symbols and Imagery*. Amsterdam: North-Holland Publishing Company, 1976.

Jacobi, Jolande. *The Psychology of C. G. Jung.* London: Yale University Press, 1973 [1942].

Jung, C. G. "Archetypes of the Collective Unconscious." In *The Collected Works of C. G. Jung.* Vol. 9i. Ed. G. Adler, M. Fordham, W. McGuire, & H. Read. Trans. R. F. C. Hull. Princeton, NJ: Princeton University Press, 1954, § 1-86.

_____. "Mind and Earth." In *The Collected Works of C. G. Jung.* Vol. 10. Ed. G. Adler, M. Fordham, W. McGuire, & H. Read. Trans. R. F. C. Hull. Princeton, NJ: Princeton University Press, 1931, § 49-103.

_____. "On Psychic Energy." In *The Collected Works of C. G. Jung.* Vol. 8. Ed. G. Adler, M. Fordham, W. McGuire, & H. Read. Trans. R. F. C. Hull. Princeton, NJ: Princeton University Press, 1928, § 1-130.

_____. "Symbols of the Mother and of Rebirth." In *The Collected Works of C. G. Jung.* Vol. 5. Ed. G. Adler, M. Fordham, W. McGuire, & H. Read. Trans. R. F. C. Hull. Princeton, NJ: Princeton University Press, 1956, § 300-418.

_____. "The Detachment of Consciousness from the Object." In *The Collected Works of C. G. Jung.* Vol. 13. Ed. G. Adler, M. Fordham, W. McGuire, & H. Read. Trans. R. F. C. Hull. Princeton, NJ: Princeton University Press, 1957, § 64- 71.

_____. "The Dual Mother." In *The Collected Works of C. G. Jung.* Vol. 5. Ed. G. Adler, M. Fordham, W. McGuire, & H. Read. Trans. R. F. C. Hull. Princeton, NJ: Princeton University Press, 1956, § 464-612.

_____. "The King and the King's Son." In *The Collected Works of C. G. Jung.* Vol. 12. Ed. G. Adler, M. Fordham, W. McGuire, & H. Read. Trans. R. F. C. Hull. Princeton, NJ: Princeton University Press, 1943, § 434-436.

_____. "The Syzygy: Anima and Animus." In *The Collected Works of C. G. Jung.* Vol. 9ii. Ed. G. Adler, M. Fordham, W. McGuire, & H. Read. Trans. R. F. C. Hull. Princeton, NJ: Princeton University Press, 1950, § 20-42.

Moore, Tom. "Artemis and the Puer." In *Puer Papers.* Irving, TX: Spring Publications, 1979, pp. 169-204.

Neumann, Erich. *The Great Mother.* Princeton: Princeton University Press, 1955.

Rilke, Rainer Maria. *Letters to a Young Poet.* New York: W.W. Norton & Company, 1962 [1934].

Stewart, R. J. "Merlin, King Bladud, and the Wheel of Life." In *The Book of Merlin.* Ed. R. J. Stewart. Poole, England: Blandford Press, 1987.

von Franz, Marie-Louise. *An Introduction to the Psychology of Fairy Tales.* Zurich, Switzerland: Spring Publications, 1973.

_____. *Problems of the Feminine in Fairytales.* Dallas, TX: Spring Publications, 1972.

_____. *The Psychological Meaning of Redemption Motifs in Fairytales.* Toronto: Inner City Books, 1980.

Walker, Barbara G. *The Woman's Encyclopedia of Myths and Secrets.* San Francisco: Harper Row, 1983.

Index

SPRING JOURNAL BOOKS

The book publishing imprint of *Spring Journal,*
the oldest Jungian psychology journal in the world

STUDIES IN ARCHETYPAL PSYCHOLOGY SERIES
Series Editor: Greg Mogenson

Collected English Papers, Wolfgang Giegerich
 Vol. 1: *The Neurosis of Psychology: Primary Papers Towards a Critical Psychology,* ISBN 978-1-882670-42-6, 284 pp., $20.00
 Vol. 2: *Technology and the Soul: From the Nuclear Bomb to the World Wide Web,* ISBN 978-1-882670-43-4, 356 pp., $25.00
 Vol. 3: *Soul-Violence* ISBN 978-1-882670-44-2
 Vol. 4: *The Soul Always Thinks* ISBN 978-1-882670-45-0

Dialectics & Analytical Psychology: The El Capitan Canyon Seminar, Wolfgang Giegerich, David L. Miller, and Greg Mogenson, ISBN 978-1-882670-92-2, 136 pp., $20.00

Northern Gnosis: Thor, Baldr, and the Volsungs in the Thought of Freud and Jung, Greg Mogenson, ISBN 978-1-882670-90-6, 140 pp., $20.00

Raids on the Unthinkable: Freudian and Jungian Psychoanalyses, Paul Kugler, ISBN 978-1-882670-91-4, 160 pp., $20.00

The Essentials of Style: A Handbook for Seeing and Being Seen, Benjamin Sells, ISBN 978-1-882670-68-X, 141 pp., $21.95

The Wounded Researcher: A Depth Psychological Approach to Research, Robert Romanyshyn, ISBN 978-1-882670-47-7

The Sunken Quest, the Wasted Fisher, the Pregnant Fish: Postmodern Reflections on Depth Psychology, Ronald Schenk, ISBN 978-1-882670-48-5, $20.00

Fire in the Stone: The Alchemy of Desire, Stanton Marlan, ed., ISBN 978-1-882670-49-3, 206 pp., $22.95

Honoring David L. Miller

Disturbances in the Field: Essays in Honor of David L. Miller, Christine Downing, ed., ISBN 978-1-882670-37-X, 318 pp., $23.95

The David L. Miller Trilogy

Three Faces of God: Traces of the Trinity in Literature and Life, David L. Miller, ISBN 978-1-882670-94-9, 197 pp., $20.00

Christs: Meditations on Archetypal Images in Christian Theology, David L. Miller, ISBN 978-1-882670-93-0, 249 pp., $20.00

Hells and Holy Ghosts: A Theopoetics of Christian Belief, David L. Miller, ISBN 978-1-882670-99-3, 238 pp., $20.00

The Electra Series

Electra: Tracing a Feminine Myth through the Western Imagination, Nancy Cater, ISBN 978-1-882670-98-1, 137 pp., $20.00

Fathers' Daughters: Breaking the Ties That Bind, Maureen Murdock, ISBN 978-1-882670-31-0, 258 pp., $20.00

Daughters of Saturn: From Father's Daughter to Creative Woman, Patricia Reis, ISBN 978-1-882670-32-9, 361 pp., $23.95

Women's Mysteries: Toward a Poetics of Gender, Christine Downing, ISBN 978-1-882670-99-XX, 237 pp., $20.00

Gods in Our Midst: Mythological Images of the Masculine—A Woman's View, Christine Downing, ISBN 978-1-882670-28-0, 152 pp., $20.00

Journey through Menopause: A Personal Rite of Passage, Christine Downing, ISBN 978-1-882670-33-7, 172 pp., $20.00

Portrait of the Blue Lady: The Character of Melancholy, Lyn Cowan, ISBN 978-1-882670-96-5, 314 pp., $23.95

More Spring Journal Books

Field, Form, and Fate: Patterns in Mind, Nature, and Psyche, Michael Conforti, ISBN 978-1-882670-40-X, 181 pp., $20.00

Dark Voices: The Genesis of Roy Hart Theatre, Noah Pikes, ISBN 978-1-882670-19-1, 155 pp., $20.00

The World Turned Inside Out: Henry Corbin and Islamic Mysticism, Tom Cheetham, ISBN 978-1-882670-24-8, 210 pp., $20.00

Teachers of Myth: Interviews on Educational and Psychological Uses of Myth with Adolescents, Maren Tonder Hansen, ISBN 978-1-882670-89-2, 73 pp., $15.95

Following the Reindeer Woman: Path of Peace and Harmony, Linda Schierse Leonard, ISBN 978-1-882670-95-7, 229 pp., $20.00

An Oedipus—The Untold Story: A Ghostly Mythodrama in One Act, Armando Nascimento Rosa, ISBN 978-1-882670-38-8, 103 pp., $20.00

The Dreaming Way: Dreamwork and Art for Remembering and Recovery, Patricia Reis and Susan Snow, ISBN 978-1-882670-46-9, 174 pp. $24.95

Living with Jung: "Enterviews" with Jungian Analysts, Volume 1, Robert and Janis Henderson, ISBN 978-1-882670-35-3, 225 pp., $21.95.

Terraspychology: Re-engaging the Soul of Place, Craig Chalquist, ISBN978-1-882670-65-5, 162 pp., $21.95.

Psyche and the Sacred: Spirituality beyond Religion, Lionel Corbet, ISBN978-882670-34-5, 288 pp., $23.95.

How to Order:

Write to us at: Spring Journal Books, 627 Ursulines Street # 7, New Orleans, Louisiana 70116, USA

Call us at: (504) 524-5117

Fax us at: (504) 558-0088

Visit our website at: www.springjournalandbooks.com